# Blender Game Development Tutorial

Dedicated to college students, independent developers and small teams who want to start their own business

*Author: Liu Liqun*

## Author Bio

He graduated from the Department of Electronic Engineering of University of Electronic Science and Technology of China in 1991, majoring in telemetry and remote control, but found that his main interest was in the field of software development and showed a high talent, so he took the path of independent developer without any hesitation.

He had independently developed a 3D game engine and used his own 3D game engine to develop and publish the casual game "3D Safari Park" for iPad in Apple App Store.

He had developed an editor extension plugin "Mantis LOD Editor" for Unity Engine to simplify 3D models, which is very popular among users.

He had developed the heavyweight "Voxel Heat Diffuse Skinning" add-on and the very best-selling "Better FBX Importer & Exporter" add-on for Blender, helping Blender to get out of the island of game development by himself.

In this book, the author describes in detail how to use Blender instead of 3ds Max and Maya for the game development workflow, and learners can focus on one area of the workflow according to their interests.

Each chapter ends with a series of entrepreneurship classroom topics, where the author relates the experiences and lessons learned in his twenty years of independent development, pointing out the pitfalls that independent developers and small teams tend to encounter, and giving straightforward solutions.

By studying this book, you will find that financial freedom is not unattainable for independent developers if you do well enough.

Whether you are a graduating college student, an independent developer just starting out, or a small team with little money, you can learn from this book and help your business succeed.


Liu Liqun

CEO of Nanjing Mesh Online Software Technology Co., Ltd.

www.mesh-online.net

# Preamble

I've been diving silently in the Zhihu website, and unintentionally answered a question about Blender, which attracted the attention of Editor Tian Zhiyuan from Publishing House of Electronics Industry. He enthusiastically sent me a copy of the Chinese version of "Learning Blender A Hands-On Guide to Creating 3D Animated Characters, Third Edition", which was just published in April 2022, and asked me to review and correct it, so I realized that I was regarded as a so-called "Guru", and I felt really flattered.

When I was lying in bed at night, I thought - I have accumulated a lot of experience and lessons during my years of independent development, which are called "Know How" in English, and they are all secret things. On the contrary, most of the success courses that can be taught in public are flashy rhetoric. The lecturers are very smart people, good at learning and passing on knowledge, but most of them can't start their own businesses. How else would Warren Buffett's lunch be worth so much? A few words from a master may enlighten you and show you the way.

So I got the idea to write this book, if I can combine my experience as an independent developer to write a tutorial on Blender game development, it should fill the gap in this area.

It's true that Blender used to be unsatisfactory and couldn't cooperate with other softwares, so it was reduced to an island of game development. For a long time, 3ds Max and Maya ruled the game development workflow. Fortunately, with the efforts of many grassroots Blender developers, the old pattern has been broken.

Many people still don't know that Blender can support the full game development workflow now.

This book describes the workflow of Blender game development from the perspective of an independent developer, including character modeling, character skinning, character animation, and character exporting, with each area containing a variety of solutions from free to paid. Learners can focus on one area according to their interest, and if they do well enough, achieving financial freedom is not an unattainable thing.

After learning this book, they will master the workflow of Blender game development and learn a lot of entrepreneurial experience that others don't talk about. Others may say, "So what if you learn it? Does anyone want you when hiring? I hope they can proudly say, "I don't care, my dream is to become an independent developer and work for myself in the future." A society where everyone strives to be a civil servant has no future; entrepreneurs are the elite of society and the hope of the future.

I would like to dedicate this book to college students, independent developers and small teams who wish to start their own business. I hope that these future social elites can unlock the confusion in their minds, take less detours on the road to entrepreneurship, bravely follow their hearts and realize their dreams.

Note: This book contains blend files and video tutorials (File Format:mp4,Resolution:3840x2160), please visit https://www.mesh-online.net/blender-game-development-tutorial.zip to download the zip file.

# Catalog

VIII

# Chapter 1 Introduction to Blender

## What is Blender?

First I will explain what is "3D", "3D" is the abbreviation of "Three Dimensional" in English, in layman's terms is non-flat. Because most users have been accustomed to directly use "3D", rather than "Three Dimensional", I also directly use "3D" instead of "Three Dimensional" in this book.

Blender is a free and open source 3D modeling, animation and rendering software, which is developed and maintained by the Blender Foundation. Anyone can get the source code of Blender for free, find bugs and fix them by themselves, or submit bugs to the Blender developers to fix them. Bugs are fixed very quickly, usually within a few days.

## Blender Extreme Start

The official website of Blender is "www.blender.org". Enter this URL in the address bar of your web browser will navigate you to Blender's website, click the "Download" button on the home page to download the latest version of Blender.

After installing Blender, start Blender, the first thing that appears in front of you is a welcome screen, click anywhere outside the welcome screen with your mouse, the welcome screen will disappear and it only displays the main interface of Blender.

In the middle of the main interface of Blender, you will see a cube with a camera on the left and a light on the top right.

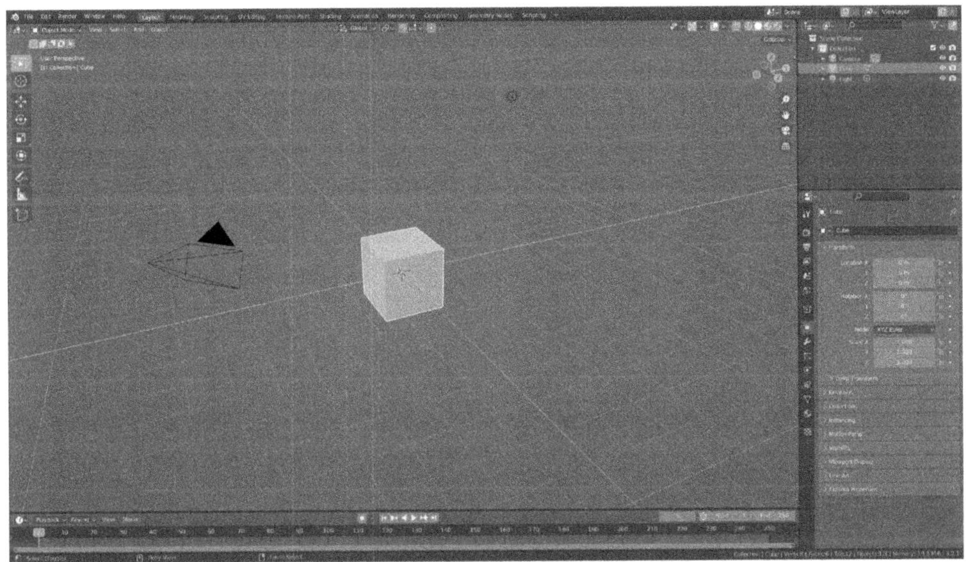

The interfaces in Blender, except for the menu bar at the top and the status bar at the bottom, is a combination of completely tiled windows, unlike other 3D softwares.

Other 3D softwares generally use a hierarchical windows design, which look hierarchical and the windows are neatly stacked according to the hierarchy, but it requires frequent switching of windows when working, which reduces work efficiency.

While Blender's design concept is to have all the windows arranged flat and presented to the user at the same time. This completely flat design looks a bit cluttered, but works efficiently.

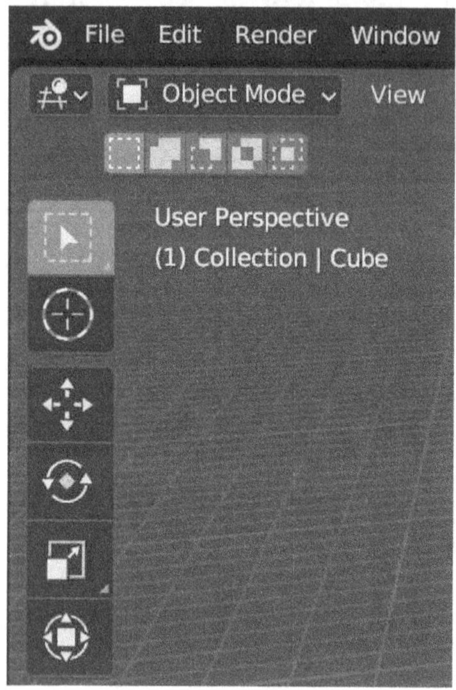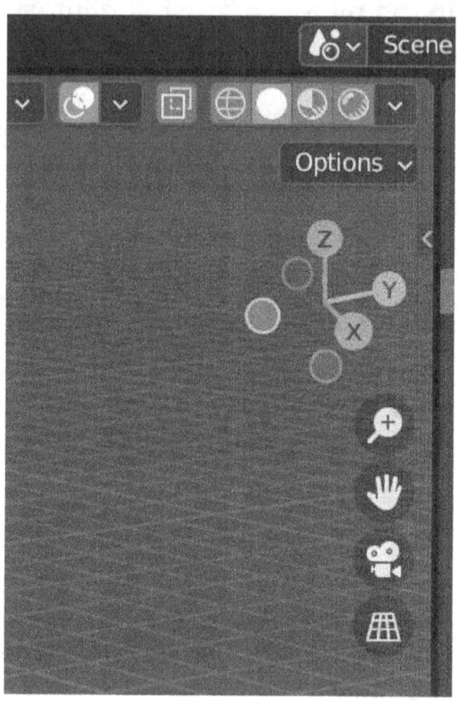

Blender's windows are designed to be universal. In the upper left or lower left corner of the window is a window type drop-down box, click on it to select another window type, and change the window type to change from one window to another, very magical.

The left side of the "3D View" is the toolbar, the third icon with four small arrows is the pan icon, click it to switch to "Pan" mode, the "Pan Controller" will appear on the object, you can use the mouse to drag the handles of the "Pan Controller" to pan the object; the fourth icon is the rotate icon, click it to switch to "Rotate" mode, the "Rotate Controller" will appear on the object, you can use the mouse to drag the handles of the "Rotate Controller" to rotate the object; the fifth icon is the zoom icon, click it to switch to "Zoom" mode, the "Zoom Controller" will appear on the object, you can use the mouse to drag the handles of the "Zoom Controller" to zoom the object.

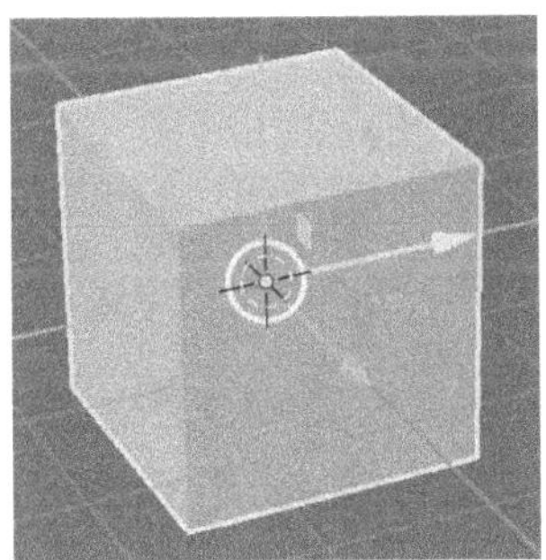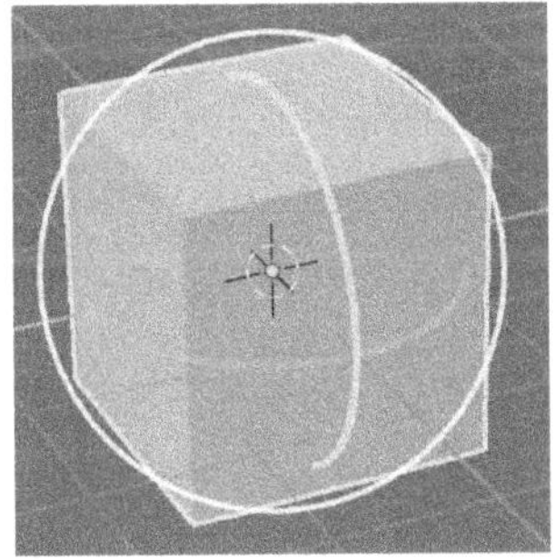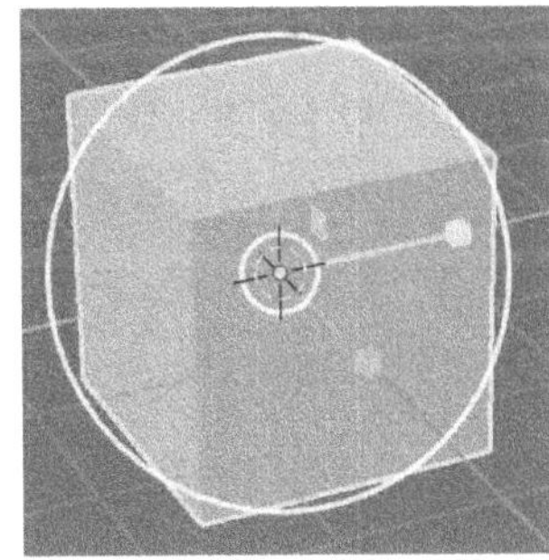

The right side of the "3D View" is the view controller bar, the first icon consists of three axes, this is the "View Rotation" controller, hold it and drag the mouse to rotate the view; the second icon is a magnifying glass, this is the "View Zoom" controller, hold it and drag the mouse to zoom the view; the third hand-shaped icon is the "View Pan" controller, hold it and drag the mouse to pan the view.

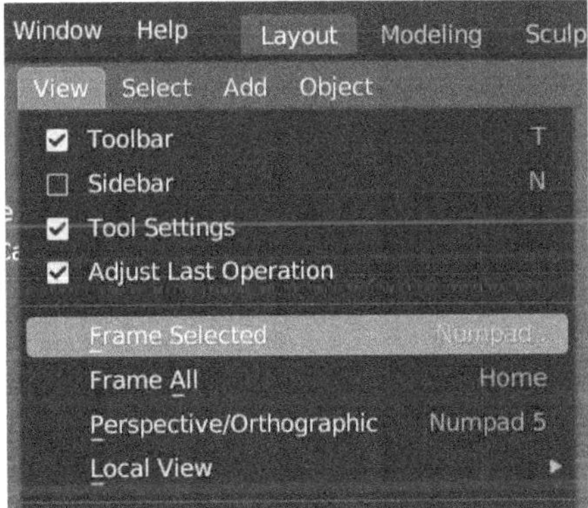

If you want to focus the view on an object, you can select it by clicking on it with the left mouse button and then execute the menu

"View -> Frame Selected" to make the object the focus of the view, and if you rotate the view, you will find that you are rotating around the object.

Once you have mastered these basic operations, you can continue with this book. If you want to learn more advanced techniques, such as how to use shortcuts with the mouse for more efficient operations, you can read the official documentation or search for "Blender for Beginners" on the YouTube website.

If you are a beginner in Blender, you can just use Blender's default layout to do anything you want. For example, if you want to view and set the material of an object, you can temporarily change the type of the middle 3D window to "Shader Editor" and this window will become a material editor. When the material is set, you can change the window type back to "3D Viewport". I also basically just use Blender's default layout to work by switching window types, which is a universal lazy working method.

For advanced users, Blender offers the ability to customize the layout by splitting and merging windows. But I don't think it's necessary for beginners, because Blender already provides some presets for common layouts, you can find them on the right side of the menu bar at the top, the current default layout is "Layout", just click with your mouse on other layout presets, such as the "Animation" layout preset, you can switch to the layout suitable for animation, very convenient.

## Why don't Big Companies Use Blender?

You may be wondering, if Blender is so good, why do so few big companies use it? There are several reasons.

1. Big companies are well-funded, the money for purchasing software accounts for only a small percentage of the company's overhead, so they prefer to spend money on expensive paid software from commercial companies, rather than trust the free software maintained by the community. In their minds, free is the most expensive. For big companies, the cost of time is much greater than the cost of purchasing software.

2. Early Blender software, the operating habits of the user interface were very unfriendly, such as the use of the right mouse button to select objects, and rely heavily on shortcuts, beginners often feel crashed after the initial attempt and give up.

3. Blender's design basically does not take into account the collaborative workflow of the team, functional but not precise, in a particular workflow, the function is not as good as commercial software, after all, commercial software is designed for teamwork.

4. The long-term formation of user habits, as the early big companies are using 3ds Max and Maya, forming a de facto industry standard, the later big companies also have to use the same software in order to easily exchange models and animations with their peers.

## Why is Blender More Suitable for Independent Developers and Small Teams?

These disadvantages of Blender happen to be advantages for independent developers and small teams: Independent developers and small teams are not worth their time, can spend more time learning complex and hard-to-use interfaces, and usually do not need to exchange models and animations with their peers; all the jobs are done in one software. So until now, Blender has been used almost exclusively by independent developers and small teams.

## Why is Blender 2.8 a Watershed Moment?

The developers of Blender were so confident that they stubbornly insisted on using the right mouse button to select objects, believing it to be the best design, and made it the default setting for the software. Although after Blender 2.5, users could switch to left mouse button object selection through customization, it was not until Blender 2.8 that the developers reluctantly made left mouse button object selection the default setting of the software.

Don't underestimate such a small change. Beginners can eventually try to explore the software features by themselves without feeling crashed. What's more, Blender 2.8 has better menus and toolbars, so even if you can't remember the shortcuts, you can still operate through the menus and toolbars. Coupled with the introduction of Blender 2.8's very eye-catching EEVEE rendering engine for high-quality WYSIWYG real-time rendering, many independent developers and small teams were curious to experience the effects of Blender's world-first high-quality real-time rendering, and since then Blender's user base started to grow rapidly.

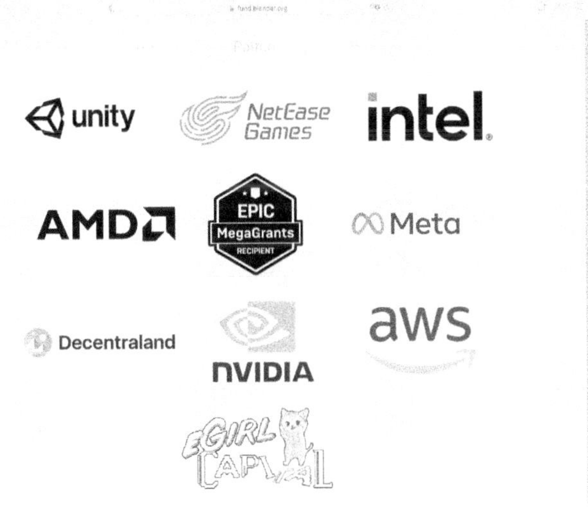

Microsoft, Google, Amazon, Meta (Parent company of the famous Facebook), Oracle, Apple, Ubisoft, Intel, Reallusion (Company that develops iClone software and Character Creator software), Adobe (Developer of PhotoShop software), AMD, NVIDIA, Unity, Epic Games (Developer of the Unreal Engine) and NetEase Games, are among the industry giants that see the potential for Blender's user growth potential and have joined the Blender Foundation. The endorsement of the big companies in turn gave confidence to independent developers and small teams who were on the sidelines and started trying to introduce Blender into the game development workflow.

In addition to the efforts of Blender developers and the strong sponsorship of industry giants, there is another group that cannot be ignored, and they are the many grassroots Blender developers who are active in the Blender Market, enriching Blender with their full-time or amateur developed 3D models, materials, animations, e-books, video tutorials and useful add-ons, and at the same time earning significant income, making an important contribution to getting Blender out of the island of game development.

For example, an auto-binding add-on named "Auto-Rig Pro", which was developed by Lucas from France, has occupied the Blender Market rankings for years, bringing considerable income to its developer.

Another example is another important add-on that I developed independently - "Better FBX Importer & Exporter", which is also highly appreciated by users, allows Blender users to exchange 3D models and animations with other softwares through native FBX add-on.

So, Blender 2.8 is a watershed moment, where everything is falling into place, things are moving in a good direction and a strong trend is forming. We all know that it's easy to succeed with the trend, so hopefully we can grasp this trend and do something about it.

## Should I Focus on One Area or be a Full-Stack Developer?

Although this book discusses the whole workflow of Blender game development, you can focus on only one area you are good at in the whole workflow of game development according to your situation, and if you do it well enough, you can survive and get a foothold.

Take myself as an example, although I had developed a 3D game engine and a casual game on iPad with it, I realized that I was lack of passion for game development and I don't like to play games, so I focus on my expertise in programming and algorithms, and choose to develop useful plugins on Unity platform and Blender platform to provide useful tools for other game developers. The income I got was much more than if I had developed the games myself.

So, the path for independent developers is broad, you can do whatever you like and what you are good at. For example, some people have good art skills, they can focus on the modeling field; some people have a good sense of action, they can focus on the animation field; some people are interested in game logic, they can focus on the game planning field; some people are good at programming, they can focus on game programming; some people like to learn and share, they can focus on making tutorials and become knowledge disseminators; some people are good at all aspects, and they can be a full-stack independent game developer.

But few people are good at all aspects, even if you are only good at one area, you can still play your own specialties, and share your achievements to others at the same time to get a significant income, and this is the typical survival path for independent developers.

## Entrepreneurship Class

---

### It Turns Out that Big Companies also Have Weaknesses

Big companies generally trade money for time.

The approach of big companies is to build a strong team, consume a lot of money in a short period of time to make a product quickly, then bring it to market quickly, and if it does not meet market expectations, they will not hesitate to cut the project and look for the next one.

Why is this so? It's cost-driven.

Big companies have high operating costs, so they must be quick.

The weakness of big companies is that they cannot fight a protracted battle.

### It Turns Out that Independent Developers also Have Advantages

Maybe you don't know it yet? Independent developers also have a big advantage over big companies.

The biggest advantage of independent developers is that they can trade time for money.

Assuming you start a business from your own home, even if you only earn a few hundred dollars a month, you will be able to survive and last a few years without a problem.

The cost for independent developers can be compressed very low and thus stick around for a long time.

Independent developers have the advantage of being able to fight a constant battle.

## I can Beat Big Companies with the Weak

Realizing the two points mentioned above, you can play to the strengths of independent developers to beat the big companies.

Don't believe me? I'll give you an example of my own.

Back then, I had developed an editor extension plugin "Mantis LOD Editor" for Unity Engine to simplify 3D models. The biggest competitor at that time was a product of a big company, whose name I won't mention. This product of mine is like an ant compared to an elephant, it is not comparable to it at all.

Most of Unity's developers are independent developers and small teams, so they are more price sensitive. Since this big company had priced its product very high, naturally it sold less, so the total revenue of this product was not high. It also had a free online service used to attract potential users. Users could upload their 3D models to its website and then wait in the queue for offline processing in the backend of the website, sometimes waiting for hours without returning the results, which was not a good user experience. It had attracted a lot of bad reviews because it couldn't get the results in real time.

Unity developers have limited purchasing power and are a typical niche market. This revenue is not a problem to support an independent developer or a small team, but it is unlikely to support a big company.

The final result was unexpected. A few years later, I found out that this big company's product had disappeared from the Unity Asset Store, and it turned out that it had been acquired by Microsoft and snowed out of existence, unfortunately disappearing in the course of time.

And after a long period of continuous iterative improvement, my product has slowly turned into the best product in this field, being selected by the editors of the Unity Asset Store for every promotion and reaping wave after wave of promotional dividends.

I hope my practical experience can bring you some confidence, big companies really have nothing to fear.

When you first start a business you are like a bicycle racer, you should go to a bicycle track to race, not to a car track to compete with cars for speed. If you choose the right track, you will find that bicycles can fly on a small track while cars can't run at all on a small track.

The secret of beating the big companies is to choose the right track.

# Chapter 2 Character Modeling

## What is 3D Character Modeling?

"Modeling" is short for "creating a model".

3D character model, generally refers to 3D human model or animal model, or anthropomorphic model of other 3D objects, such as the car model in "Cars" and the robot model in "RoboCop".

3D character modeling is to create the 3D character models you need from scratch, such as 3D human models, 3D animal models, and anthropomorphic 3D object models.

In addition to 3D character modeling, 3D modeling also includes the design of other 3D objects in the scene, such as 3D terrain, 3D models of tables, chairs and benches, also called environment modeling.

## Advantages and Disadvantages of Modeling by Yourself

The advantage of modeling by yourself is that you can design any characters you like at will. But modeling by yourself is very difficult for most independent developers, because modeling is not just as simple as learning how to operate the software, just like you have learned to draw lines on paper with a pencil, you still can not draw a character sketch.

To turn from a novice to an artist, you need to have sketching skills, or even sculpting skills to do modeling by yourself, which requires a long time of practice and accumulation, but also a little artistic talent.

If you find that you are not artistically talented enough, don't be discouraged because there are now softwares that can automatically generate 3D character models, for example, from photos, to generate very realistic 3D character models in a few minutes.

There are also some 3D softwares dedicated to making characters, such as the free "MakeHuman", the paid "Character Creator", and the meta-universe image generating website - "Ready Player Me", which can customize various parameters and then generate custom 3D characters with one click, which is very convenient.

You can also go to Blender Market, Unity Asset Store and Unreal Marketplace to buy ready-made 3D models, which are very diverse and basically meet the requirements of independent developers.

If you are not satisfied with any ready-made 3D models, you can also go to some websites that take outsourcing tasks to post modeling tasks and ask professional 3D modelers to help you customize paid 3D models.

The topic of 3D modeling is so big that it could write a book by itself. So this book, as a Blender game development tutorial, will not be about how to do modeling, but will only focus on other workflow besides modeling.

If you want to learn modeling, you can buy other books, such as "Learning Blender A Hands-On Guide to Creating 3D Animated

Characters, Third Edition", and learn slowly with its video tutorials, or search for "Blender Modeling" on the YouTube website, follow the domestic or foreign Blender "Gurus" to learn modeling.

For most independent game developers, it is more common to import ready-made 3D models instead of modeling by themselves, or to hire professional 3D modelers to outsource the modeling workflow for game development, and it is easier to make things work.

When I was developing the casual game "3D Safari Park" for iPad, 3D models of all animals were ready-made. Nowadays, there are a wide variety of 3D models available in the Unity Asset Store, which can be bought very cheaply. I imported the purchased 3D models of the animals into Maya LT subscribed from the Steam Store, designed the skeleton, painted the vertex weights manually, made keyframe animations, exported them as FBX files, and finally imported them into my own 3D game engine. Although I knew nothing about modeling, the keyframe animations I made were also very naive, at that time I didn't even know IK, could only use FK rotating joints to make keyframe animations, but it did not prevent this game could be on the Apple App Store and bring me income for more than ten years.

So it's not hard to make a game independently, but the hardest thing is what happens after you have made the game.

When you are excited to publish the game you have spent months to make, and after a few days, you find that the number of downloads is almost zero, do you feel that months of hard work has been wasted?

Everyone says that entrepreneurship is a narrow escape game. In my opinion, this statement is not true - when you don't understand something, you always feel that the future is unknowable and life is like rolling the dice. For people who see things for what they are, God never rolls the dice. The reason you feel that the future is lost is because you don't yet understand how it works.

In future chapters of the entrepreneurship class, I will continue to lead you to gradually recognize the laws of independent developers in the entrepreneurial process and teach you how to make use of your strengths and avoid weaknesses to improve the success rate of your business.

## Generate Character Models with MakeHuman

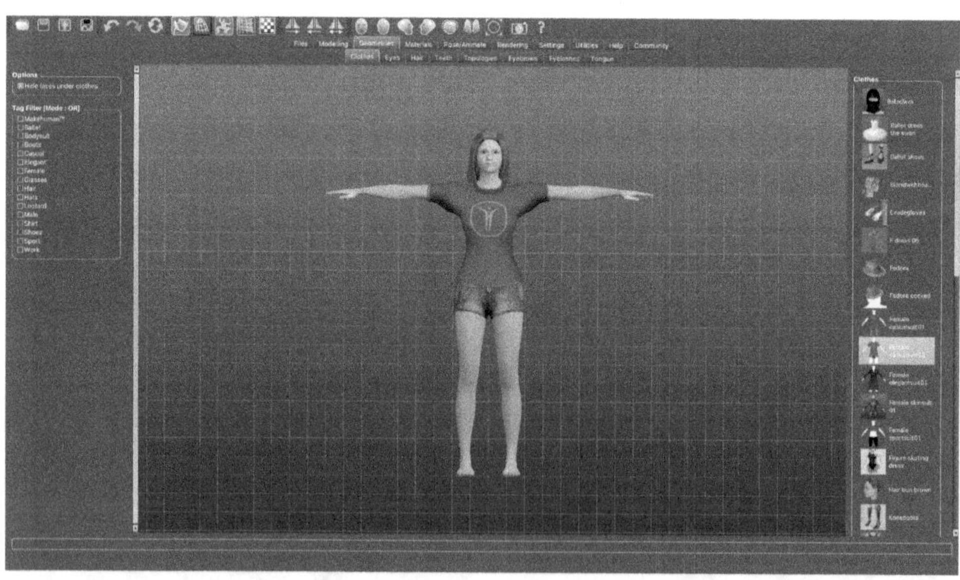

"MakeHuman" is a free foolproof 3D character modeling software. Drag the mouse to adjust the parameters, you can adjust the height of the character, and then choose the style of eyes, eyebrows, hairstyle, hat, clothes and shoes for the character, and you can design a good-looking 3D character model within minutes.

This free software is maintained by community volunteers. The software is not updated frequently and can only meet basic design needs. If you need to generate more personalized 3D characters, you may need to use other software instead.

## Generate Character Models with Character Creator

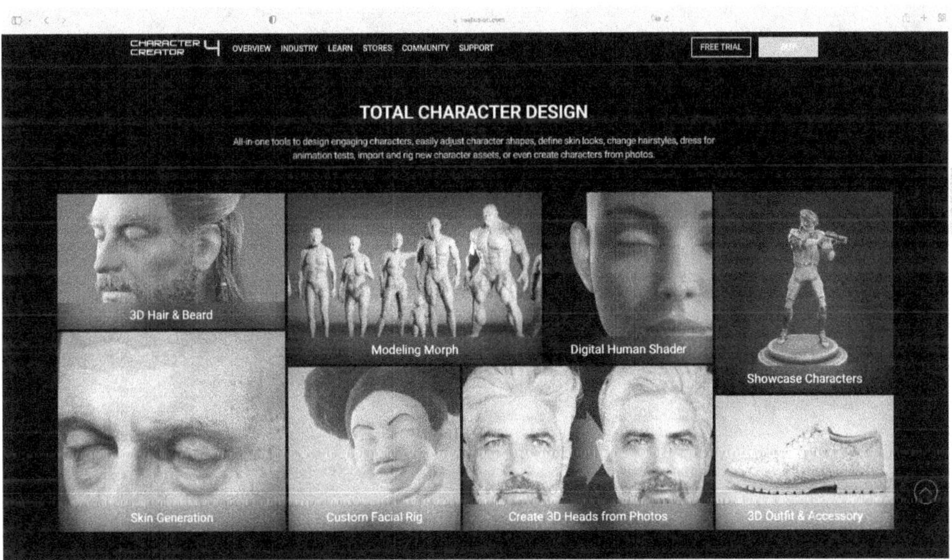


If you have sufficient budget, you can buy the paid "Character Creator" software at a price of $300 for the basic version, or double the price if you want to buy the "Character Creator Digital Human Essential Bundles" for up to $600. This software has more adjustable parameters and can be customized for a more personalized 3D character model.

## Generate Character Models with Ready Player Me

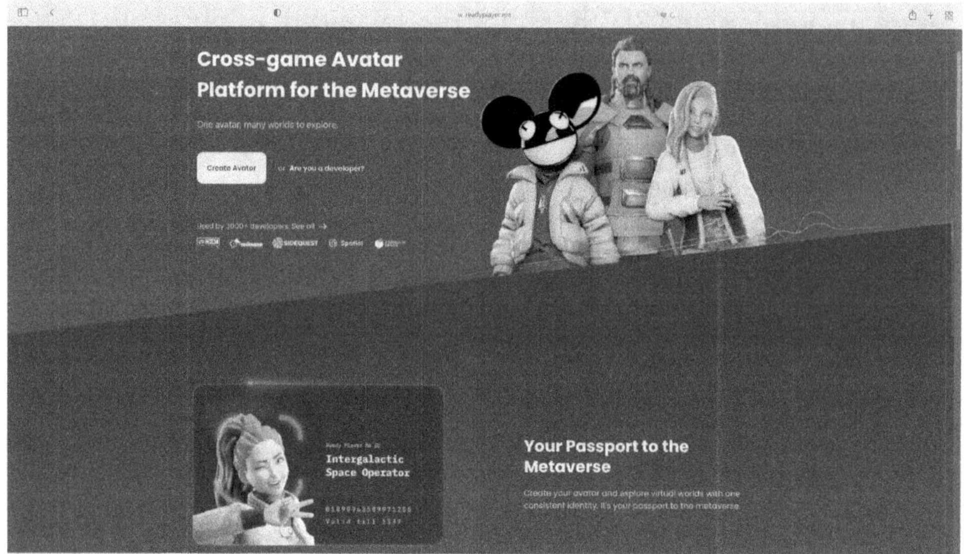


"Ready Player Me" is a meta-universe image generating website that generates 3D character models in a cartoon style that can be used as a unified image for the meta-universe world.

The 3D characters generated by this website can be imported into Blender, and plugins are also provided to import directly into Unity Engine and Unreal Engine.

The product is free for developer partners who have registered on its website. Since the meta-universe concept has been a big hit in the past two years, it may continue to be free for quite a long period of time. This product is currently in the stage of rapidly developing users with the power of capital, so I wish it can find a profit model in the future and be able to survive and continue to provide free cartoon character customization services to everyone.

## Generate Character Models from a Real Photo

There is a popular research topic in the field of machine learning on how to generate 3D models from a single photo, and there are already relatively good results and experimental products.

For example, the aforementioned paid "Character Creator" software has a plug-in called "Headshot", which is artificial intelligence-driven and can generate a 3D character model from a photo and can be fine-tuned on top of that to get a 3D character model that is not exactly the same as the real photo.

By generating 3D character models based on real photos, social celebrities can make their real images into images in the meta-universe, thus replicating the celebrity effect in reality directly into the meta-universe and continuing to gain celebrity worship in the meta-universe.

For ordinary people, they prefer to hide their real image and socialize in the meta-universe with their own mental perfect image or exaggerated personalized cartoon image. So I think it makes little sense for the ordinary people to generate images in the meta-universe that are exactly the same as their own.

## Purchase Character Models from Major Resource Stores

There are several major resource stores where you can buy ready-made 3D models, and the websites I frequently visit are -

Turbosquid, Hum3d, Unity Asset Store, Unreal Marketplace, and Blender Market.

After purchasing a 3D model, you can use it directly in your game or import it into Blender to make some simple personalized changes; if it is a static 3D model, you also need to add bones to it, bind the model, make animations, and finally export it to your game for use.

At present, the Unity Asset Store has the most abundant 3D models, the prices are moderate; and the 3D models of Unreal Marketplace are generally more expensive, of course, the qualities are also very high, maybe most of the users of Unreal Engine are team users, more concerned about the quality rather than the price.

If you want to buy commercial Blender models, you can go to Blender Market, which is the most professional Blender resource store I know. Besides 3D models, you can also find PBR materials, e-books, video tutorials, and a variety of powerful and useful add-ons.

# Entrepreneurship Class

---

## This Elementary School Math Problem is not Simple

In elementary school, there is a math problem about inlet pipe and outlet pipe in a pool.

Problem: A pool has an inlet pipe and an outlet pipe. If only the inlet pipe is opened, the pool can be filled up in 2 hours, and then the pool can be emptied in 6 hours by closing the inlet pipe and opening only the outlet pipe.

Question: How long can the pool be filled from an empty pool if we open the inlet pipe and the outlet pipe simultaneously?

Solution: Let the volume of the pool is 1, then the water inlet speed is 1/2 (1 hour into 1/2 pool of water), the outlet speed is 1/6 (1 hour to drain 1/6 pool of water).

Time = Volume / (Inlet Speed - Outlet Speed) = 1 / (1/2 - 1/6) = 3 (hours)

Answer: It takes 3 hours to fill up.

Can you see any entrepreneurial mysteries in this classic elementary school math problem?

## The Formula to Break the Curse of the Narrow Escape Game

Many people say that entrepreneurship is a narrow escape game, Mr. Li Ka-shing certainly do not believe.

Mr. Li Ka-shing has long cautioned entrepreneurs to always maintain adequate cash flow, but inexperienced entrepreneurs generally do not pay attention to it, the reason for the failure of entrepreneurs who were shot dead on the beach is almost always the capital chain rupture.

Look again at the above formula for calculating the elementary school math problem.

Time = Volume / (Inlet Speed - Outlet Speed)

If you compare entrepreneurship to the problem of water storage in a pool, time is the time to achieve wealth freedom, the volume is the wealth expectation, the inlet speed is the speed of earning money, the outlet speed is the speed of spending money.

Then, the above formula becomes:

Time to Achieve Wealth Freedom = Wealth Expectation / (Speed of Earning - Speed of Spending)

It doesn't matter if the denominator is smaller, it's just a slower growth of wealth, but don't turn negative, a negative number means you're not far from the capital chain rupture. Conversely, if your capital consumption is always less than the capital replenishment, you can never go out of business, it's as simple as that.

The biggest advantage of independent developers is the low cost. When you feel difficult, cut all unnecessary expenses, live first, use time to polish your product, slowly wait for your highlight moment to come.

## Digging for Gold or Selling Shovels?

In the era of the "Great American Gold Rush", many people who dug gold did not earn money, but the people who sold shovels made money.

You must have thought of a key question, is it possible to make money by making games?

The essence of whether you can make money by making games is a simple business question: if the revenue is greater than the overhead, you can make money; conversely, if the overhead is greater than the revenue, you cannot make money.

The bad news is that there are too many games nowadays, and game users are so dazzled by the huge number of games that you may not be able to make any waves when you put a lot of effort into developing a game and throwing it into the market.

The good news is that the success of your game is determined by the end game users, and if they like your game, your game will be successful, even if you are an independent developer or a small team.

For example, in the Apple App Store, many games from big companies with seemingly good quality don't sell well because they can't be the best in their category and users only play the best one; there are also small games from grassroots developers that sell well, such as "Flappy Bird", because of its simple, fun, challenging and addictive.

The situation now is that independent developers and small teams that go off the beaten path are prone to success, while conventional practices do not work as well.

For example, some small and micro teams use rapid development, rapid publishing approach to minimize costs, although the quality of the games are not high, but the number of games is large, they can also earn money by going.

Some small teams take the opposite approach to the above, and only make one high-quality game polished with a lot of effort, and the preview version just released is a sensation in the world, and it can be expected that the official release will be a big success.

A few game teams have transformed from personally developing games to providing paid technical services for other game teams, such as providing high-precision 3D character modeling services, similar to the practice of selling shovels in the "Great American Gold Rush" era.

Generally speaking, making games focuses more on sufficient capital and correct operation, and technology is rather secondary; while providing peripheral services for games focuses more on excellent technology, and capital and operation are rather secondary.

Therefore, whether to dig gold or sell shovels needs to be comprehensively decided according to one's own interests, funds and technical capabilities.

# Chapter 3 Character Skinning

## What is Character Skinning?

Nowadays, the mainstream 3D modeling technology only models the outer contours of the character, and the 3D model is made up of meshes of the outer contours. If a virtual skeleton matching the shape of the 3D model is placed inside the 3D model, the 3D character is like a skin covered on the virtual skeleton, which can move with the movement of the virtual skeleton, so that's how the term "Skinning" comes.

Character skinning is the fusion of a 3D character model with a virtual skeleton using some algorithm, just like the relationship between bones and flesh in our body. When the character skinning is completed, the flesh attached to the bones will follow the bones and move.

## How Many Kinds of Character Skinning are There?

Character skinning in Blender is both easy and painful. It's easy because Blender has built-in automatic skinning command; it's painful because Blender's built-in automatic skinning command often fails.

For example, when you build a virtual skeleton for a 3D character model, you select both the 3D character model and the virtual skeleton and execute Blender's built-in automatic skinning command. You think that it should be a thing as simple as a snap, but then Blender pops up a window telling you: "Bone Heat

Weighting: failed to find solution for one or more bones". Translated into layman's terms, this means, "Sorry, I tried my best, but I regret to inform you that the automatic skinning has failed!"

As a novice, are you confused? Such a smart computer does not know how to do skinning, what should I do as a novice? Do I have to learn to be a painter, take a brush and paint the vertex weights on the 3d character model by hand little by little?

The vertex weight refers to the extent to which the skin is driven by the bones, indicating which small piece of skin will follow the movement of one or several bones. The larger the vertex weight, the more it is driven by the bones; conversely, the smaller the vertex weight, the weaker it is driven by the bones.

Back in the day I was on Maya LT, there was no good tool to automatically generate vertex weights, so I really painted the vertex weights manually. It is very troublesome to paint the vertex weights by hand, and after I paint more skillfully, I can paint a model completely in about half an hour.

More than a decade has passed, is there a better way now?

The answer is: "Yes". Various algorithms have been invented to automatically generate vertex weights.

The first algorithm, which simulates the diffuse process of heat on the surface of a model, can get very good detailed vertex weights, but it works poorly on the overlapping part of the model.

The second algorithm, which simulates the diffuse process of heat in the volume of the model, can get very good overall vertex weights, but poor results for the detailed parts of the model.

The third algorithm, which simulates real skin tension with spring dynamics and dynamically calculates the vertex weights, can get a very good dynamic skinning result, but cannot be used for traditional skeletal animation.

Each of the above three methods has its own advantages and disadvantages, and the best way is to use them in combination.

## Simple Robotic Rigid Body Skinning

In robotic rigid body animation, there is no transition between the motions of the parts, and the motions of the parts on both sides of the joint belongs to one side only; while in organic body animation, there is a smooth transition between the motions of the parts, and the skin on both sides of the joint is deformed by smooth transition.

The skinning of robotic rigid body is the simplest, and it can be done without any skills, here are the steps:

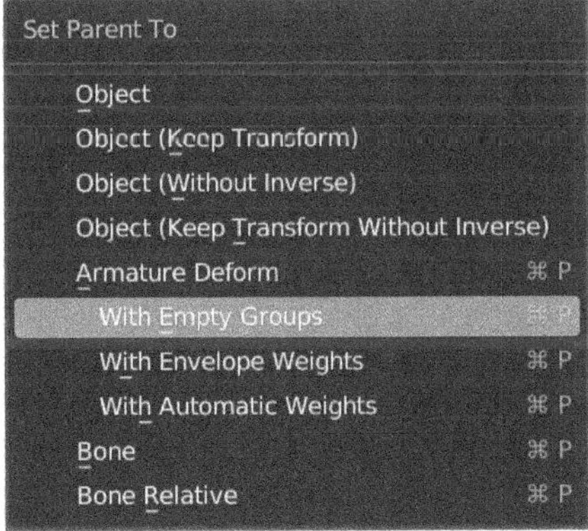

In the first step, select all parts of the robot in the "3D View", finally hold down the "Shift" key, click to select the armature, press the "Ctrl + P" key and select "Armature Deform -> With Empty Groups" in the pop-up menu. This command skins all parts of the robot to the armature and automatically generates a set of empty vertex weights.

In the second step, if the body parts of the robot are independent, select one of the body parts in the "3D View", press the "Tab" key to enter "EDIT" mode, press the "A"  key to select all the vertices; if the body parts are not independent, select the whole body in the "3D View", enter "EDIT" mode, and select all the vertices of one of the body parts.

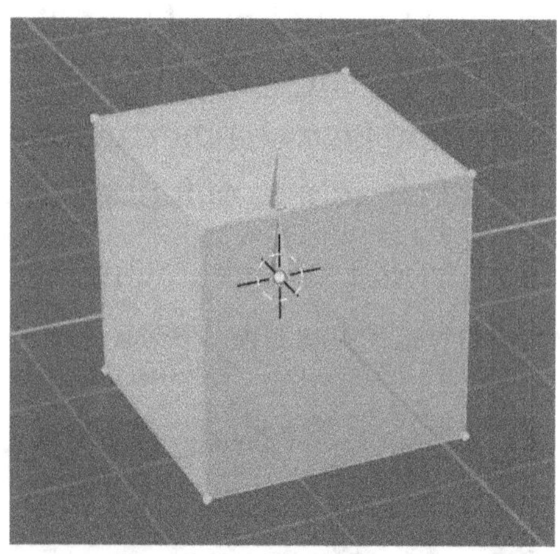

In the third step, select the name of the bone to drive this body part in the "Properties -> Object Data Properties -> Vertex Groups", make sure the "Weight" value is the default 1.0, and then click the "Assign" button, the weights of all vertices of this body part will be assigned a value of 1.0, which means that the body part is fully driven by this bone.

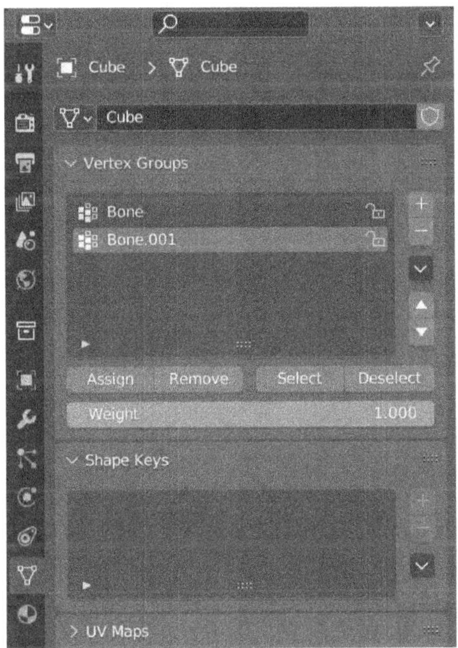

Repeat steps 2 and 3 to assign drive bone to each body part until all body parts are driven by the corresponding bones, and the robotic rigid body skinning is complete.

## Classic Surface Heat Diffuse Skinning

Select all parts of the 3D character in the "3D View", finally hold down the "Shift" key, click to select the armature, press the "Ctrl + P" key and select "Armature Deform -> With Automatic Weights", this command skins all the parts of the 3D character to the armature and automatically generates a set of smooth and natural vertex weights with the surface heat diffuse skinning algorithm.

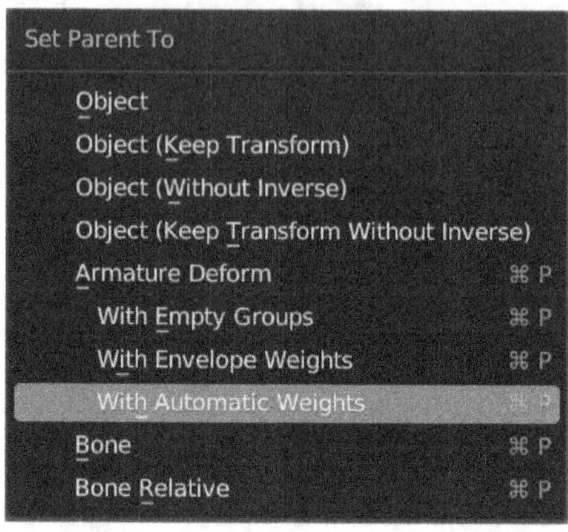


This algorithm is the most classical and can get very good skinning result on watertight manifold 3D models.

Watertight manifold means that the whole 3D model is closed, without any gap, and will not leak a drop of water when thrown into the water, and the mesh that constitutes the 3D model must be a completely regular smooth surface, without any protrusion or spliced angular traces. In layman's terms, watertight manifold means that the whole model is obtained by deforming a complete skin, you can think of it as a very elastic balloon full of air squeezed into a model by hand.

Unfortunately, actual 3D models are rarely watertight manifold, and artists do not model in this way. They are designed in the way the artists like and are good at, either modeling with polygons, sculpting, or a combination of techniques.

The algorithm does not work well on non-watertight or non-manifold 3D models, and when simulating heat diffuse, the overlapping parts cannot calculate the correct vertex weights because they do not receive the radiant heat from the armature; there is also a serious problem, the algorithm essentially finds the optimal vertex weights by solving a large system of linear equations, but sometimes the algorithm fails to find the solution for some unknown reason. Anyone who has learned equations knows that not all equations have solutions, for example, if x squared equals -1, there is no solution.

Anyway, some smart people have explored some tricks to avoid the flaws of the algorithm.

The first trick is to enlarge the 3D model and the armature simultaneously by 100 times, then do the skinning, and finally shrink the 3D model and the armature by 100 times simultaneously after the skinning is finished. Why do it this way? After checking the source code of Blender, I found that it is caused by the floating point error, especially small floating point number (less than 1e-6) will be incorrectly ignored when doing surface heat diffuse skinning, resulting in skinning failure. If we enlarge both the model and the armature by 100 times, the particularly small floating point number becomes a larger floating point number, and the algorithm works correctly. When the skinning is done, just shrink the model and armature by 100 times simultaneously to the original size. This trick can solve the problem that the skinning algorithm fails to find the solution due to floating point error when solving large linear equation systems.

The second trick is to first split the 3D model into very many small parts, in "EDIT" mode, press the "P" key and select "By Loose Parts" to split the character. Then skin these small parts to the armature, and after the skinning is completed, select all the small parts, press the "Ctrl + J" key, and then combine these small parts into a single 3D model. This trick can partially solve the problem of not being able to generate the correct vertex weights for some parts due to internal occlusion of the model.

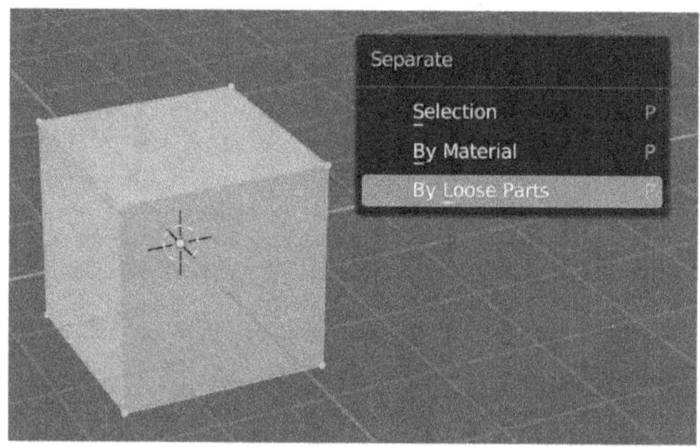


The third trick is to generate a watertight wrapping film for the character model, use this wrapping film to skin the bones on behalf of the character, and then transfer the skinning result to the character. This trick can solve the problem that the skinning algorithm fails to find a solution for some unknown reasons when solving large linear equations.

## Clever Wrapping Film Transfer Skinning

Although the wrapping film transfer skinning trick is clever, but in practice, I found that its success rate is not very high, you need to repeatedly adjust the parameters, the generated skinning result will also lose the details of the trousers seams, finger seams and other detailed parts, so we just lean about it, not recommended.

This skinning trick involves first generating a tightly wrapped film for the character model, as if the character model were vacuum-packed with plastic film tightly attached to it. Although the character model itself is not watertight manifold, the wrapping film is watertight manifold. When skinning, the wrapping film is skinned onto the armature, and after the skinning is completed, the vertex weights on the wrapping film are then transferred to the character model according to the closest distance principle. This technique can partially solve the problem of not being able to generate correct vertex weights for some parts due to internal occlusion of the model, as well as the problem of skinning failure due to some unknown reasons when the skinning algorithm cannot find a solution when solving a large system of linear equations.

The following are the steps to generate a wrapping film for a character model.

Add an empty volume object to the scene, then add a "Mesh To Volume" modifier to the volume object, select the character model as the source, adjust the "Exterior Band Width" (e.g. to 0.01) and "Voxel Amount" (e.g. to 256) to make the volume object look sharper, with slightly larger contour than the character object.

Add a Blender built-in "Cube" model to the scene, then add a "Volume To Mesh" modifier to the "Cube" model, selecting the volume object added in the previous step as the source. Select "Apply" from the modifier drop-down menu to apply the modifier and get a slightly rougher wrapping film model of the character model.

This slightly rough wrapping film model sometimes consists of two parts inside and outside, the outermost shell is closed watertight manifold; while the inside part is usually broken, usually generated by overlapping parts, this part will cause interference when skinning, so we need to delete the inside part in "EDIT" mode.

Select the wrapping film model, enter "EDIT" mode, move the mouse cursor to the model, press the "L" key, all the vertices that make up the outermost shell will be selected automatically, press the "H" key to hide them, press the "A" key to select all internal broken vertices (but sometimes you may find that no internal broken vertices are selected, which means that all vertices are on the shell, so there is no need to delete internal broken vertices), press the "X" key to delete all selected vertices. Press the "Alt + H" key to show all the hidden vertices of the shell and exit "EDIT" mode.

In the "3D View", click to select the wrapping film model that has just been cleaned up broken internal vertices, then hold down the "Shift" key and click to select the armature, press the "Ctrl + P" key and execute "Armature Deform -> With Automatic Weights", you can use the classic surface heat diffuse skinning algorithm to generate better results for the wrapping film model.

However, from a practical point of view, in the process of generating the wrapping film, the skinning may fail because the parameters are not appropriate, for example, the "Exterior Band Width" parameter of the volume modifier is set too small, causing the generated shell to have small holes, resulting in the surface heat diffuse skinning algorithm can not finding the solution. If you find that the skinning fails, you can adjust the parameters and try again and again until the skinning is successful.

After the wrapping film model is skinned successfully, you can add a "Data Transfer" modifier to the character model, select the wrapping film model as the source, activate "Vertex Data", select "Vertex Groups" and click the "Generate Data Layers" button to generate the data transfer layers. Select "Apply" from the modifier drop-down menu to apply the modifier and transfer the vertex weights from the wrapping film model to the character model.

However, the above method is not foolproof, some cases cannot be dealt with, the close vertices, such as trousers seams and finger seams and other detailed parts will stick together when generating the wrap, which will generate wrong skinning results.

## How to Install, Upgrade and Remove Add-ons?

By clicking the menu "Edit -> Preferences..." you can enter the Preferences interface, and click the "Add-ons" tab to enter the "Add-ons" management window.

Type keywords in the search box to filter out existing add-ons, click the checkbox in front of the add-on to enable the add-on, and click the checkbox again to disable the add-on.

Click the "Install..." button at the top of the add-ons tab and select the add-on you want to install in the file selection window that pops up. The add-on can be a compressed archive in "zip" format, which Blender will unzip automatically when installing it, or a Python source file with the extension "py". After a few seconds, the add-on name will appear, indicating that the add-on has been installed, but it will not be enabled automatically, you need to enable it manually by clicking the checkbox in front of it.

What if there is a new version of the add-on that needs to be upgraded? The most reliable way is to remove the old add-on first and then install the new one.

Type the keyword of the add-on name in the search box, filter out the add-on, click the small triangle in front of it to expand the details, and click the "Remove" button to completely remove the old add-on from the disk.

Then follow the previous steps to reinstall the new version of the add-on. To ensure that the add-on takes effect, you'd better relaunch Blender.

## Elegant Voxel Heat Diffuse Skinning

The voxel skinning is proposed to solve the problem of overlapping part of the surface heat diffuse skinning obscuring, since the heat diffuse along the surface of an object is obscured by the overlapping parts, wouldn't the heat diffuse along the volume not be a problem?

You can imagine the character model as a solid statue, the heat diffuses from the embedded bones and spreads along the solid statue, it will spread to any location of the model without dead ends, thus getting ideal vertex weights.

Blender Market has a paid 'Voxel Heat Diffuse Skinning' add-on, which can achieve voxel heat diffuse skinning.

However, voxel skinning solves one problem and introduces a new one. The overlap problem is solved, but details are lost, and places like finger seams are wrongly considered to be glued together, resulting in incorrect vertex weights for very detailed areas.

The good news is that the author of this voxel skinning add-on (actually me) has taken this problem into account, so this add-on supports a two-stage skinning strategy, where the first stage uses the surface heat diffuse skinning algorithm to generate vertex weights at details, and the second stage uses the voxel heat diffuse skinning algorithm to generate vertex weights at non-details, and finally the vertex weights generated in the two stages are merged together.

With two-stage skinning, you can get a perfect skinning result for both detailed parts like pants seams and finger seams, and complex overlapping parts like clothes and equipment.

Assuming you have installed this add-on, press the "N" key in the "3D View", the right sidebar will be shown, and click the "Mesh Online" tab, which is the voxel skinning add-on interface.

As you can see, the voxel skinning add-on actually contains three add-ons - the "Surface Heat Diffuse Skinning" add-on, the "Voxel Heat Diffuse Skinning" add-on, and the "Corrective Smooth Baker" add-on.

"Voxel Resolution", indicates the resolution of the voxel, the default resolution is 128, the 3D character is evenly split into 128 slices on the longest coordinate axis. The higher the resolution, the more memory it takes up. If you want to set a resolution of 1024, the

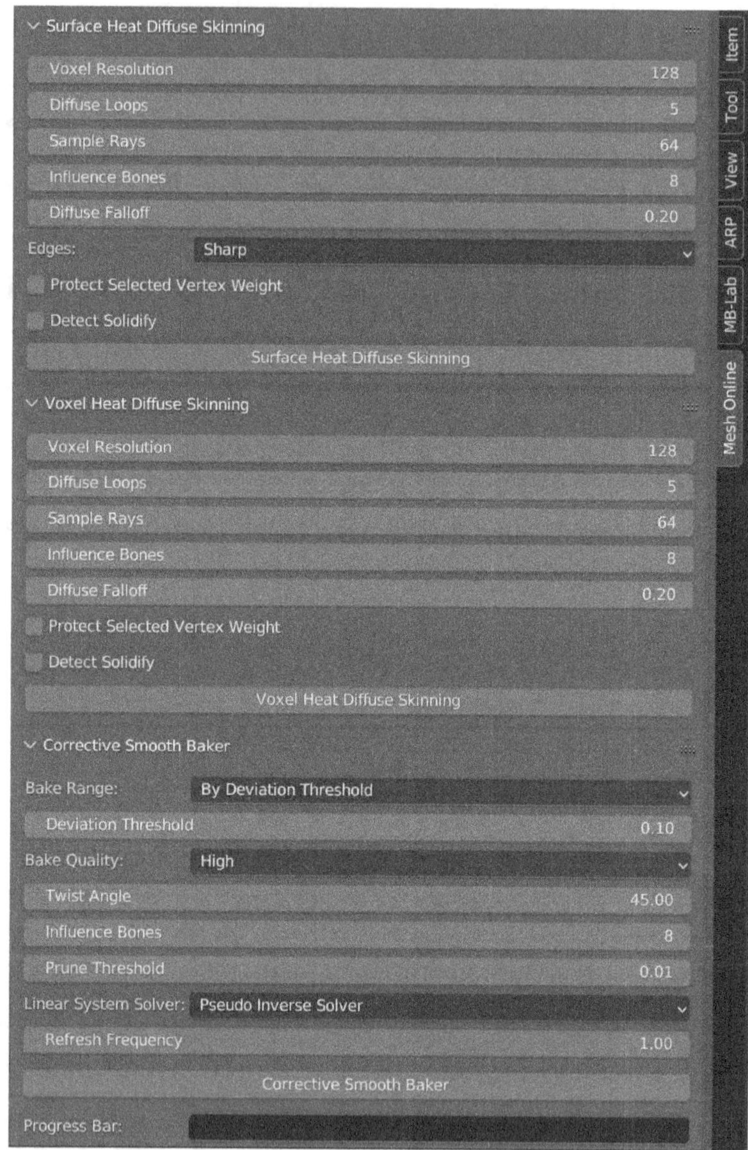


skinning process may take up more than 10G bytes of memory, and your computer needs at least 16G bytes of memory to work. Not the larger the resolution the better the skinning results, too large a resolution may cause the seams of clothes and equipment can not be completely closed, which may result in wrong skinning result. I generally recommend using the default resolution.

"Diffuse Loops", indicates how many cycles of heat diffuse, you do not need to change this value.

"Sample Rays", which indicates the number of sampled rays, defaults to 64. Higher values result in more accurate voxel shapes, but runs slower.

"Influence Bones", which indicates how many bones the vertices are controlled by, defaults to 8 for host animations; if you're animating for mobile devices, you need to reduce it, for example by setting it to 4.

"Diffuse Falloff", indicates the smoothness of the skinning transition, the larger the value the more sharp the transition, the smaller the value the smoother the transition.

"Protect Selected Vertex Weight", means protect the vertex weight of the selected vertices. You need to enter "EDIT" mode first, select some vertices, and then exit "EDIT" mode. The default value is "Disabled".

"Detect Solidify", means detect double-sided objects, if the 3D character's body, clothes or equipment have normal inward faces, please enable this option to ensure the correctness of the skinning result, when enabling this option please make sure that the armature is inside the 3D character and cannot reach outside the 3D character, otherwise the skinning result will be inaccurate. If the

3D character does not have double-sided objects, use the default value. The default value is "Disabled".

If you want to do a simple voxel skinning, select all the parts of the 3D character in the "3D View", finally hold down the "Shift" key, click to select the armature, click the "Voxel Heat Diffuse Skinning" button, the add-on will report the progress in light blue text, wait a moment, the skinning will be completed.

At any time during the skinning process, you can terminate the skinning by pressing the "ESC" key in the "3D View".

If your 3D character has detailed areas like fingers and toes, you need to use the two-stage skinning method to get perfect skinning results.

In the first step, select all the parts of the 3D character in the "3D View", finally hold down the "Shift key", click to select the armature, press the "Ctrl + P" key and select "Armature Deform -> With Automatic Weights", this command skins all the parts of the 3D character to the armature and automatically generates a set of smooth and natural vertex weights with the surface heat diffuse skinning algorithm.

In the second step, Select the 3D character in the "3D View", press the "Tab" key to enter "EDIT" mode, click on the blank space of the scene with the mouse, this will deselect all the vertices that have been selected, then click on the "Toggle X-Ray" icon to enter "X-Ray" mode. In "X-Ray" mode, the vertices will be selected together with the back vertices when you select them with the mouse. By moving, rotating and zooming the view to focus on the finger, click and drag

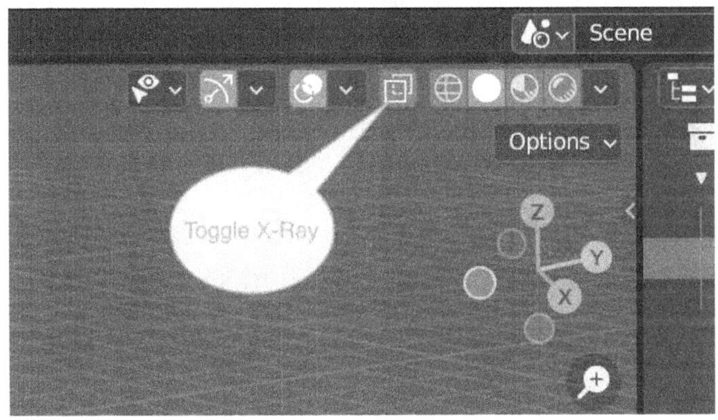


the left mouse button, the starting and ending points of the mouse path will form a diagonal rectangular box, and the vertices inside the box will be selected and highlighted in orange, selecting all vertices from the wrist to the five fingers. Then hold down the "Shift" key and drag the mouse to select all the vertices of the other hand. If there are other detailed parts, do the same and add the vertices of all the detailed parts. Click the "Toggle X-Ray" icon again to exit "X-Ray" mode. Press the "Tab" key in the "3D View" to exit "EDIT" mode.

In the third step, Click the checkbox in front of "Protect Selected Vertex Weight" on the interface of the "Voxel Heat Diffuse Skinning" add-on to enable the "Protect Selected Vertex Weight" feature. Select all parts of the 3D character in the "3D View", finally hold down the "Shift" key to click to select the armature, click the "Voxel Heat Diffuse Skinning" button, the add-on will report the progress in light blue text, wait a moment, the skinning will be completed.

With the two-stage skinning method, we can automatically skin detailed parts such as fingers and toes, as well as complex parts such as clothes and equipment, minimizing the manual work of adjusting vertex weights, providing work efficiency and saving time.

There is one more thing to mention, I once tried to completely solve the problem that Blender's built-in surface heat diffuse skinning algorithm failed to find a solution when solving large systems of linear equations due to some unknown reasons. However, after trying this, I found that this is a limitation of linear algebra itself, and there are cases that are mathematically unsolvable.

So what should we do? In engineering, we can use finite elements to solve problems that have no mathematical solution, that is, we can give up solving analytically in mathematics and simulate the real surface heat diffuse in finite element space to find the engineering solution, and we can solve the problem.

After much effort, I finally made a surface heat diffuse skinning algorithm that always has a solution and open sourced it for free on Github (https://github.com/meshonline/Surface-Heat-Diffuse-Skinning) for the benefit of other Blender users, and its skinning result is similar to that of Blender's built-in surface heat diffuse skinning algorithm. If Blender's built-in surface heat diffuse skinning algorithm fails, you can use this add-on to generate surface heat diffuse skinning results for your character model.

For the convenience of users, I have also integrated this free and open source "Surface Heat Diffuse Skinning" add-on into the "Voxel

Heat Diffuse Skinning" add-on, so you don't have to download and install it separately from Github.

Therefore, the "Voxel Heat Diffuse Skinning" add-on on Blender Market is actually a value-for-money 3D character skinning toolbox that provides users with a complete 3D character skinning solution.

## Amazing Smooth Deformer Baking Skinning

Blender has a built-in "Smooth Corrective" modifier, which uses spring dynamics to simulate real skin tension and dynamically calculate vertex weights to get a very natural deformation effect, especially for dynamically optimizing skeleton-based skin deformation.

What does it mean? If you have used the "Surface Heat Diffuse Skinning" algorithm combined with the "Voxel Heat Diffuse Skinning" algorithm to skin your character, but are still not satisfied with the skinning result, you can add a "Smooth Corrective" modifier to your character and you will find that the unnatural areas of your model's deformation will become exceptionally natural, really like the skin is deforming.

Unfortunately, this modifier works by directly modifying the position of the model vertices in real time, which you can understand as another muscle-based skinning system. When exporting the FBX file to the game engine, only the traditional skeleton-based vertex weights can be exported, and the muscle-based vertex weights will all be lost.

Blender Market has a paid "Corrective Smooth Baker" add-on (also authored by me), through which we can bake the very natural dynamic deformation effect generated by this modifier to the skeleton-based vertex weights. You can think of the baking process as using an algorithm to transfer the muscle-based vertex weights to the skeleton-based vertex weights, and after baking, we can export the optimized skeleton-based vertex weights to the game engine.

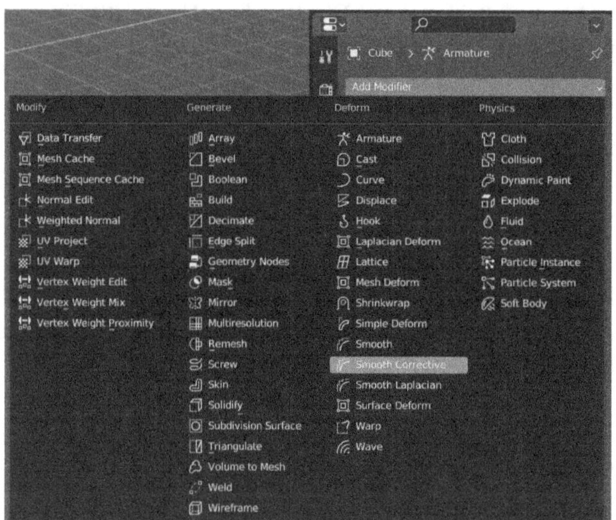
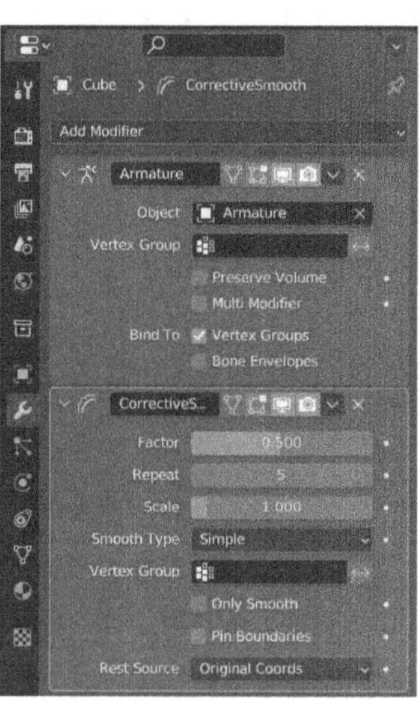

Suppose you have finished skinning your 3D character and want to optimize the skinning result further, please select the 3D character first, then click the wrench-shaped icon in the "Properties" window on the right side of Blender, which is the "Modifier" tab. Click the "Add Modifier" drop-down box at the top of the "Modifier" tab and select "Smooth Corrective" under the "Deform" category, a "Smooth Corrective" modifier will be added to the 3D character. You will also notice that the skin of the 3D character immediately becomes smoother.

Assuming you have installed this add-on, press the "N" key in the "3D View", the original hidden right sidebar will show up, click the "Mesh Online" tab, which is the "Corrective Smooth Baker" add-on interface. In the "3D View", select all the parts of the 3D character, finally hold down the "Shift" key, click to select the armature, click the "Corrective Smooth Baker" button, the character will twist quickly, then stand still, and start baking smooth deformation to the vertex weight, the progress bar below will show the baking progress. The baking time depends on the CPU performance of your computer, the number of vertices and the number of bones in the 3D character model. Baking a typical 3D character would take a few minutes on my computer if I use the default settings.

The "Bake Range" has three options: "All Vertices", "Selected Vertices", and "By Deviation Threshold".

"All Vertices", means baking for all vertices.

"Selected Vertices", means baking for selected vertices, you need to enter "EDIT" mode first, select some vertices, and then exit "EDIT" mode.

"By Deviation Threshold", means baking for the vertices which deviation value are greater than the threshold, the deviation value refers to the distance the vertex deviates from its original position under the influence of the "Smooth Corrective" modifier.

"Deviation Threshold", which indicates the threshold value in centimeters (cm), has a default value of 0.10, representing 1 mm.

There are five options for "Bake Quality": "Low", "Medium", "High", "Very High", and "Highest". The default value is "High", which means a high quality baking with medium time. If you think the baking time is too long, you can set it to "Medium" or "Low" to reduce the baking time by lowering the baking quality. If you don't care about the baking time, you can set it to "Very High" or "Highest" to increase the baking quality with a longer baking time.

"Linear System Solver", which indicates which linear system solver to use. Although the add-on provides several choices, after testing, "Pseudo Inverse Solver" is the most stable and reliable solver.

During the baking process, you can press the "ESC" key in the "3D View" to terminate the baking process at any time, because the add-on is baking the vertices with larger deviation values first, and then baking the vertices with smaller deviation values, so even if the baking is terminated early in the middle, the baking result is still acceptable.

For the user's convenience, I have integrated this "Corrective Smooth Baker" add-on into the "Voxel Heat Diffuse Skinning" add-on, so you don't have to buy it separately.

Of course if you only want to buy an independent "Corrective Smooth Baker" add-on and don't need the  "Voxel Heat Diffuse Skinning" add-on, you can buy this add-on separately with no problem at all.

# Entrepreneurship Class

## Connection is a Double-Edged Sword

The worse the legal environment of the city, the greater the role of connections, all walks of life are monopolized by connections, with connections, you can make money while lying down, without connections, you can't do anything.

But connection is a double-edged sword that can give you easy access to the market and can also be taken away at any time by someone else's more powerful connections. If you are a grassroots entrepreneur and don't have any connections, you don't have to be discouraged, you can still be successful. The way to achieve this is to choose to make products that don't depend on connections from the beginning, and you will be completely free from the shackles of connections and even achieve greater success than relying on connections.

Usually monopolistic industries are highly dependent on connections, such as electricity, environmental protection and some other industries, to make such industry products, it is difficult to step into their fields without connections; while products directly oriented to end-users are not dependent on connections, such as cell phones, foods and other industries, to make such products, just do a good job of technology and marketing and you will be successful.

Grassroots entrepreneurs are best to make end-user-oriented products, such products do not rely on connections, the marketing phase will not encounter man-made obstacles, and more likely to succeed.

## Is Fear of Competition a Coward?

Yes, fear of competition is cowardice, but it can avoid harm.

When wild animals meet, they quickly assess each other's strength and then decide whether they should attack or run away, with the weaker side choosing to run away as the wisest decision.

Independent developers and small teams are on the weaker side of the competition, and competing directly with big companies, while overwhelming, is not the best strategy. If you can avoid the competition and survive well when you are just starting out, it is a wise approach.

As you study more and more about an industry field, you can always find gaps in this industry, and gaps are everywhere for those who want to. If you can grasp the opportunity, you can make a product that can both fill the industry gap and solve the pain points of the industry, get a head start on the market, and be free to forage in the small blue ocean field you find by yourself, which is much better than fighting hard in the mature red ocean market.

Cowardice is a realm. When others are squeezing the canoe bridge, you are strolling in the courtyard.

Cowardice is a kind of wisdom. You don't have any enemies, the only thing you need to do is to surpass yourself.

# Chapter 4 Character Animation

## Is It Hard to Make Animation?

Compared to modeling, animating is much easier.

The animation process is divided into two parts - binding character and making keyframe animation.

Binding character is the character skinning described in the previous chapter.

Making keyframe animation is to put the skinned character model in different poses at appropriate time points and record them.

## Make Animation with Pure FK

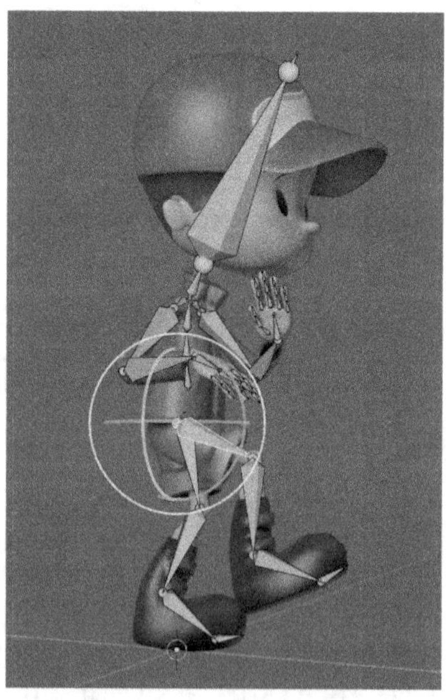

The easiest way to make animation is to rotate the bones in sequence to put the character in a pose. For example, if the character has a leg lifting action, we can rotate the thigh bone, then the calf bone, then the ankle bone to achieve the leg lifting action.

The specific operation is, In the "3D View", click the left mouse button to select the armature, press the "Ctrl + Tab" key to enter "POSE" mode, click the rotation icon in the left toolbar to enter the "Rotation" mode, click the thigh bone to rotate the thigh bone; then click the calf bone to rotate the calf bone; then click the ankle bone to rotate the ankle bone to achieve the leg lifting action.

This method is called Forward Kinematics, or FK for short. The advantage is that the rotation angle of each bone can be set precisely; the disadvantage is that it is very troublesome to pose by rotating the bones sequentially, for example, if you rotate a bone, all the children bones belonging to it will also follow the rotation, and you need to adjust the rotation angle of multiple bones repeatedly in order to place a bone in a specific position.

## Make Animation with IK

Another more efficient way to pose is to only move the end bone, which triggers a chain of bones connected to the end bone automatic move to pose. For example, let the character reach for an apple, you can move the character's wrist bone to the position of the apple, the wrist will automatically drive the forearm, the forearm will automatically drive the upper arm, and the upper arm will automatically drive the torso to adjust the character's pose.

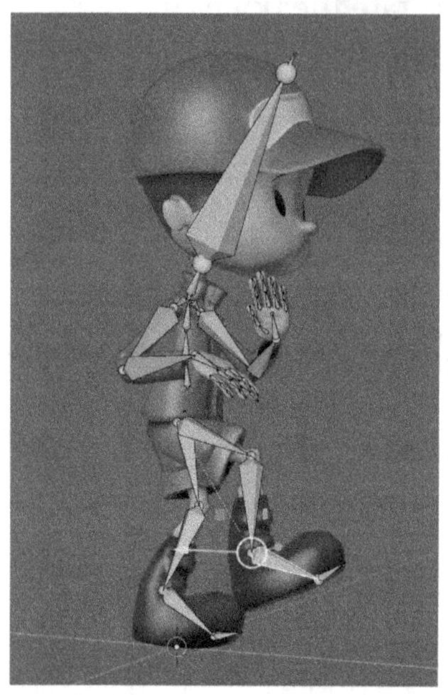 

This method is called Inverse Kinematics, or IK for short, and has the advantage of fast pose placement; the disadvantage is that the animation track is not graceful, just like pulling a marionette, which looks unnatural.

IK is achieved by constraints, in the "3D View", click the left mouse button to select the armature, press the "Ctrl + Tab" key to enter "POSE" mode, click an end bone, such as the right ankle bone, in the "Properties" interface, click the "Constraints" tab, add an "Inverse Kinematics" constraint, then set the "Chain Length" to 2 and deselect "Use Tail" option to complete the IK settings. If you move the right ankle bone, you will find that the thigh bone and calf bone will also be pulled into motion.

FK and IK have their own advantages and disadvantages, and are usually used in conjunction with each other when actually making animations. For example, we can first use IK to place a rough pose by quickly dragging a few end bones, and then use FK to fine-tune some bones to make the pose looks more graceful and the animation track looks more natural.

## Bake Cloth Simulation to Skeleton Animation

In many 3D games, you often see that the 3D character's clothes flutter naturally with the movement, and it is difficult to achieve the natural fluttering effect if you manually adjust the bone poses.

Some game engines have built-in cloth simulation, which can calculate the cloth simulation effect in real time, but the cloth simulation is very computationally intensive, which will significantly slow down the running speed of the game in mobile games and even cause game lag, so the real-time cloth simulation is only suitable for host games.

In order to reduce CPU consumption and improve the smoothness of the game, a practical approach is to do cloth simulation in Blender, and then bake the cloth simulation effect into skeleton animation to achieve the natural fluttering effect at low cost.

Blender can be used to simulate the swaying of hair, the fluttering of clothes, and even the elasticity of muscles by enabling the "Cloth" properties of any 3D models.

Assuming we've learned how to do cloth simulation, how do we bake the cloth simulation into a skeleton animation? The trick is the "Vertex Group" and the "Tracking" constraint.

In Blender, the 3D model has a "Vertex Group" property. You can think of a vertex group as a group of vertices in a 3D model divided into several groups according to their purposes. Each vertex in a vertex group has a weight, and each vertex group has a name. When interacting with other objects, the vertex group will only work if the name of the vertex group set by other objects matches it, and the weight of each vertex in the vertex group indicates how much the vertex works.

We can purposefully select some vertices in the 3D model so that the position of each selected vertex corresponds to the joint position of the bone, and generate a vertex group with a name for each selected vertex.

Then add a "Tracking" constraints to each bone in "POSE" mode, in the parameters of the tracking constraint, set "Target" to the 3D model, and set "Vertex Group" to the name of the vertex group where the vertex in the corresponding position is located. This is equivalent to binding the bone joints to the vertices in the corresponding positions.

When the cloth is simulated, the 3D model will be driven by the cloth simulation system to generate a very natural fluttering effect, and the vertices on the 3D model will drive the bone joints to do the same movement.

Finally, we use Blender's built-in bones animation baking command to bake the passive motion of the bones into keyframe animation, so that even if all tracking constraints are removed, the bones will be driven by the keyframe animation; turn off the cloth simulation on the 3D model, bind the 3D model to the bones, and the skeleton animation will drive the 3D model. At this point we can export the skeleton animation to the game engine and use the skeleton animation to achieve a natural fluttering effect.

## Make Animation with Blender's Free Built-in "Rigify" Add-on

If you are just learning Blender animations or don't like to use third-party add-ons, you can use Blender's built-in free auto-binding add-on.

Whether it is FK or IK, you need to select a bone first, then rotate or move this bone, due to the number of bones, to select which bone needs to be carefully selected among so many adjacent bones, a little carelessness may choose the wrong bone, so the direct manipulation of bones in the production of animation is not efficient.

For this reason, almost all 3D animation software introduces the concept of "Controller", which is a customized special shape to represent one or more bones, while the bones themselves are hidden and only the corresponding controllers are displayed on top of the body of the 3D character model, which is very visual and intuitive. It is much easier to manipulate a 3D character through a controller than through a bone, which can significantly improve the efficiency of making animation.

Rigify is a free built-in animation add-on of Blender, it is disabled by default, search for "rigify" in the "Edit- > Preferences... - > Add-ons" interface to find it and enable it. It can automatically generate a rig with controllers for 3D characters, which is a great tool for animation.

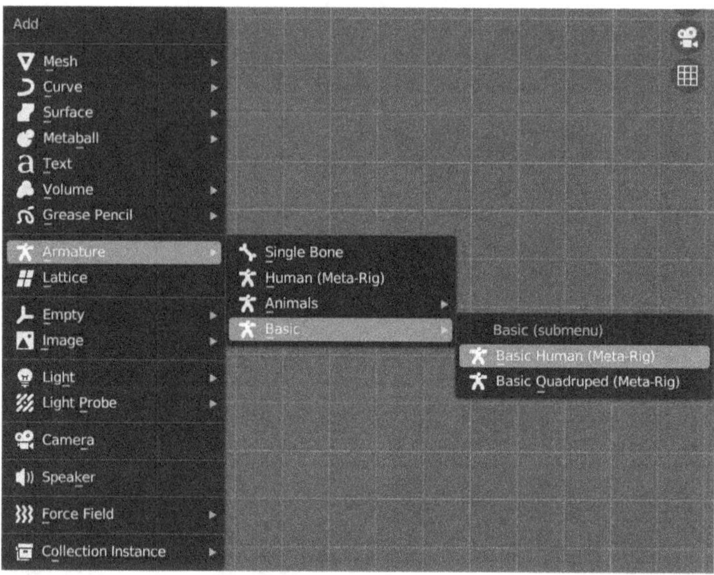

In the "3D View", press the "Shift + A" key, and from the pop-up menu, select "Armature -> Basic -> Basic Human (Meta-Rig)", a basic human meta-rig will be added to the scene.

This add-on is purely manual bone alignment when binding 3D characters, press the "Tab" key to enter "EDIT" mode and adjust the position of each bone one by one. If the model is symmetrical, you

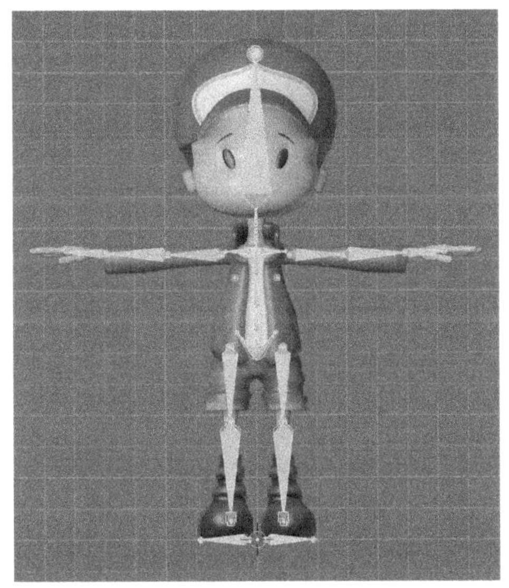

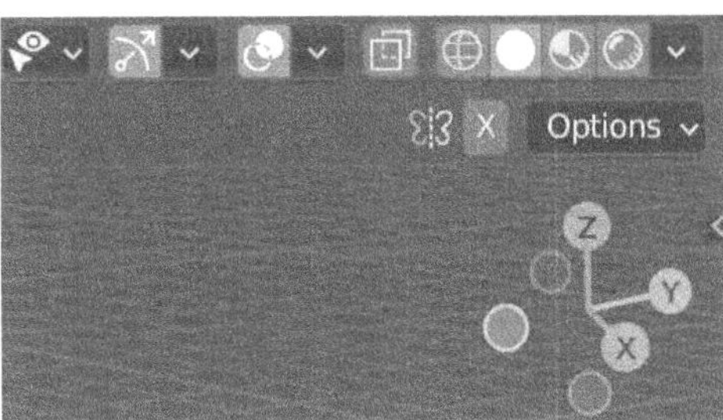


can also click on the "X" icon located in the upper right corner of the window to enable mirror mode, adjusting only one side of the bones, the other side of the bones will also follow the movement. However, since the 3D character only needs to be bound once, and you can enjoy the automatically generated controllers once the binding is done, it is worth the extra time.

After the meta-rig is aligned, click the "Skeleton" tab in the "Properties" window on the right, scroll the mouse wheel, find the "Rigify" section, and click the "Generate Rig" button to generate a rig with controllers.

Rigify can generate character controllers not only for humanoid characters, birds and quadrupeds, but also for any character. This is because Rigify is modular in design, you can build complex meta-

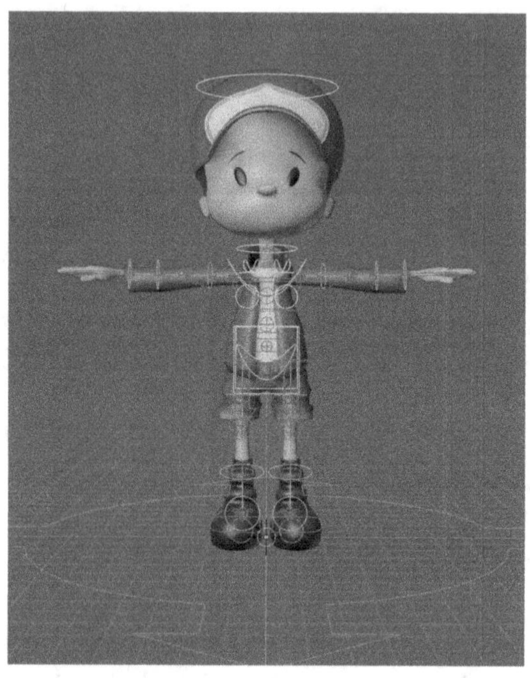

rig by combining meta modules, and then generate rig with controllers from the meta-rig.

Select the meta-rig, press the "Tab" key in the "3D View", enter "EDIT" mode, click the "Skeleton" tab in the "Properties" window on the right, scroll the mouse wheel, find the "Rigify" section, expand the "Samples" section, and you can see all the meta modules provided by Rigify.

The Rigify add-on offers 27 meta-modules:

Basic catalog, copy bones chain (basic.copy_chain)

Basic catalog, pivot (basic.pivot)

Basic catalog, raw copy bone (basic.raw_copy)

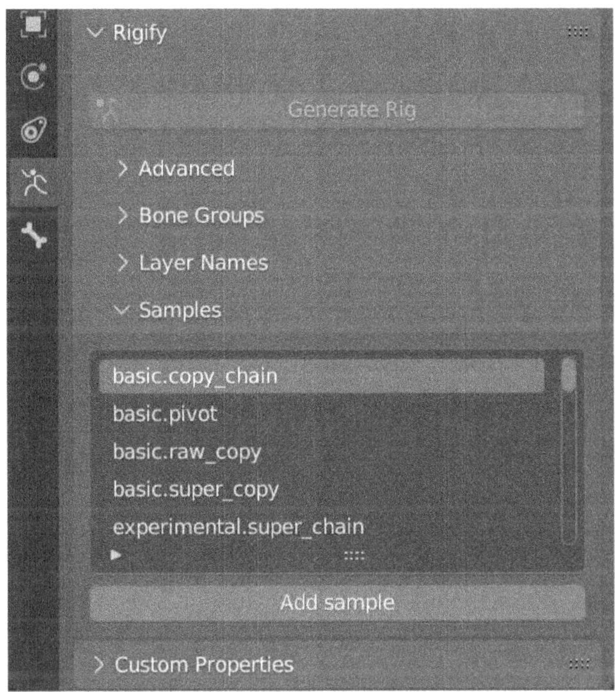

Basic catalog, super copy bone (basic.super_copy)

Experimental catalog, super bones chain (experimental.super_chain)

Face catalog, basic tongue (faces.basic_tongue)

Face catalog, eyes (faces.skin_eye)

Face catalog, chin (faces.skin_jaw)

Face catalog, face bone (faces.skin_face)

Limb catalog, upper limbs (limbs.arm)

Limb catalog, front paws (limbs.front_paw)

Limb catalog, lower limbs (limbs.leg)

Limb catalog, paws (limbs.paw)

Limb catalog, hind claws (limbs.rear_paw)

Limb catalog, simple tentacle (limbs.simple_tentacle)

Limb catalog, super finger (limbs.super_finger)

Limb catalog, super limbs (limbs.super_limb)

Limb catalog, super palm (limbs.super_palm)

Skin catalog, anchor (skin.anchor)

Skin catalog, basic bones chain (skin.basic_chain)

Skin catalog,  glue (skin.glue)

Skin catalog, stretchy bones chain (skin.stretchy_chain)

Skin catalog, transformation group, basic (skin.transform.basic)

Spines catalog, basic spine (spines.basic_spine)

Spines catalog, basic tail (spines.basic_tail)

Spines catalog, super head (spines.super_head)

Spines catalog, super spine (spines.super_spine)

If you are proficient in these meta-modules, you can build any complex Rigify meta-rig and then generate a rig with controllers in one click.

The best way to become proficient in these meta-modules is to analyze existing prefabricated meta-rigs.

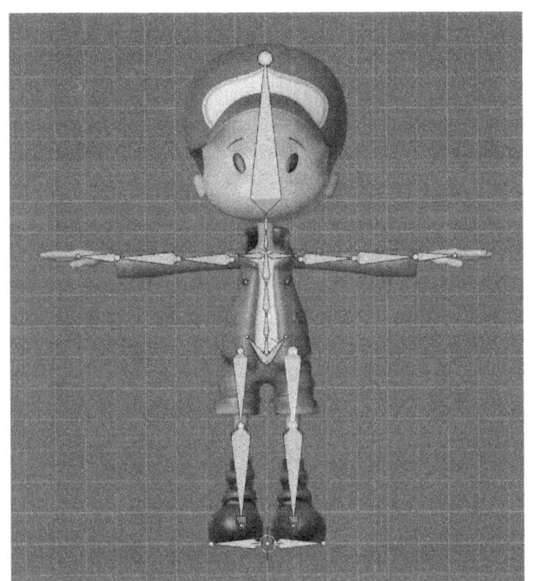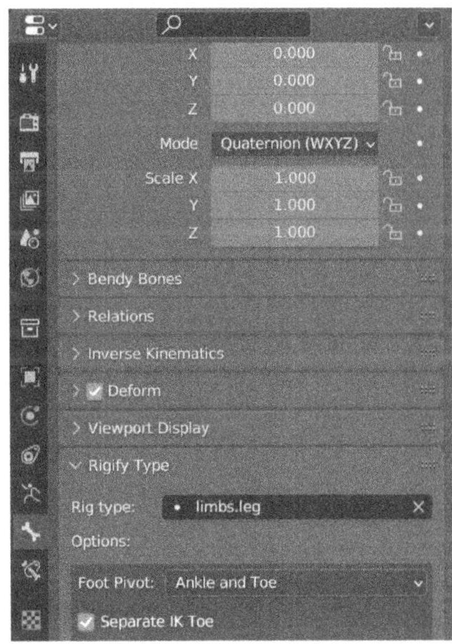

Take the above example of the basic human meta-rig. Click on the meta-rig and press the "Ctrl + Tab" key in the "3D View" to enter "POSE" mode. Click on the left thigh bone, click on the "Skeleton" tab in the "Properties" window on the right, scroll the mouse wheel, find the "Rigify Type" section, expand it, there is a "Rig type" item, its value is "limbs.leg", which means it is a limbs catalog, lower limbs; If you click on the left upper arm bone, the value of "Rig type" is "limbs.arm", which means it is a limbs catalog, upper limb; if you click on the first spine, the value of "Rig type" is "spines.basic_spine", which means it is a spines catalog, basic spine; if you click on the first neck bone, the value of "Rig type" is "spines.super_head", which means it is a spines catalog, super head; if you click on the left shoulder bone, the value of "Rig type" is "basic.copy", it means this is a basic catalog, super copy bone, that is, a single bone; if you click on the left hip bone, the value of "Rig type" is "basic.super_copy", it means this is a basic catalog, super copy bone, which is also a single bone. All these meta-modules are combined into a complex meta-rig through a simple hierarchical relationship.

You can also go on to analyze other prefabricated rigs provided by Rigify, such as the meta-rigs of birds, horses, cats, sharks, and wolves, to understand how these complex meta-rigs are assembled from basic meta-modules.

Due to the length limitation, this book cannot cover all the Rigify meta-modules in detail. If you are interested in Rigify's meta-modules, you can find tutorials about Rigify by searching the "Rigify" keyword on the Blender Market website.

I personally recommend two video tutorials - "Rig Anything With Rigify" and "Rigify Skeleton Rigging", the author's explanation is very comprehensively, covering almost all the details of the Rigify add-on.

After generating the rig with controllers, you first need to bind the 3D character to the rig with controllers, you can use Blender's built-in surface heat diffuse skinning algorithm, or you can use the more advanced voxel two-stage skinning algorithm, this chapter will not go into the specific steps of skinning.

Once the character skinning is done, it's easy to make animations. Click on the rig, press the "Ctrl + Tab" key in the "3D View" to enter "POSE" mode, trying to move the red-colored IK controller, you will find that the character moves like a marionette; trying to rotate the green FK controller, you will find that the green FK controller rotates, but the character does not follow. This is because the character is controlled by IK by default, you can press the "N" key to display the right sidebar, click the "Item" tab, find "Rig Main Properties", click "IK -> FK "button, the character's IK controller will be snapped to the FK controller, and the character's movements will be synchronized with FK. If you want to permanently use FK instead of IK, you can change the value of "IK-FK" from 0.0 to 1.0. A value between 0.0 and 1.0 means that IK and FK work proportionally simultaneously, the smaller the value, the greater the role of IK, the greater the role of FK.

If you have learned how to manipulate the controller, you can create keyframe animations. The easiest way to do this is to turn on automatic keyframe recording. Clicking on the little "Dot" shaped button at the bottom of the "Timeline" window activates the auto-record keyframe feature, and when you make poses at various time points, the poses will be automatically recorded.

For advanced users, Blender also has a built-in non-linear animation editor that allows you to merge many of the simple animation sequences you create to form more complex animations, such as combining two animations of running and jumping into a running first then jumping animation, or turning a uniform speed animation into a variable speed animation with two fast ends and a slow middle, just like the common slow close-up motion in movies.

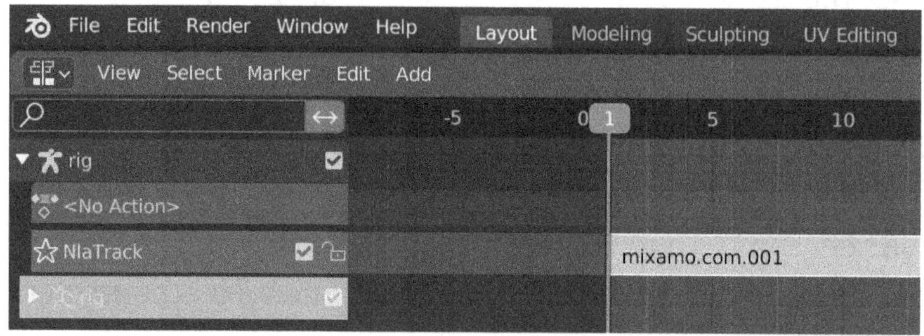


Because the non-linear animation editor is the content that advanced users need to master, this book will not explain in depth. This book is mainly for beginners, now that you are able to learn this chapter, to learn the non-linear animation editor by yourself should not be a problem.

Because the skeleton hierarchy of Rigify is extremely complicated, Blender's free built-in FBX add-on cannot export the correct FBX file for game engines. You can find a few solutions on GitHub, but none of them are very stable and reliable, as most of them use hard-coding to reorganize the skeleton hierarchy, and if the Rigify version is upgraded, these methods may fail to work.

To export your Rigify animations to a game engine, you can purchase the "Better FBX Importer & Exporter" add-on from Blender Market, a powerful native FBX importer and exporter that can export generic Rigify character animations to a generic game engine in one click. This means that either biped creatures, quadrupeds, or custom strange creatures can be exported to Unity

Engine, Unreal Engine, Godot Engine, or your own customized engine and have the animations in FBX load and run correctly.

## Make Animation with the Paid "Auto-Rig Pro" Add-on

Auto-Rig Pro is a paid auto-binding add-on developed by French developer Lucas, which is more powerful than Blender's built-in Rigify add-on.

This add-on is actually a toolbox for animation, containing many functions, with skeleton semi-automatic alignment function, when binding the model, you can save a lot of time manually adjusting the positions of the bones; there is also an enhanced auto-skinning function, its complex, optimized skinning process generates better skinning results than the skinning results obtained by directly running the auto-skinning command; also contains an "Animation Retargeting" module; this add-on also supports exporting FBX files that generate customized engine compatible skeletons for Unity Engine and Unreal Engine.

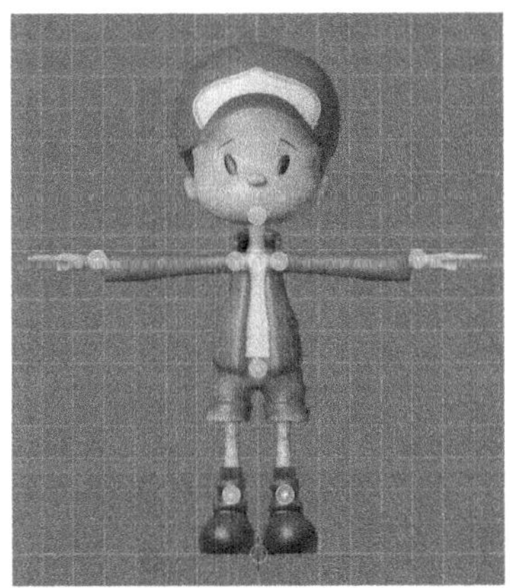
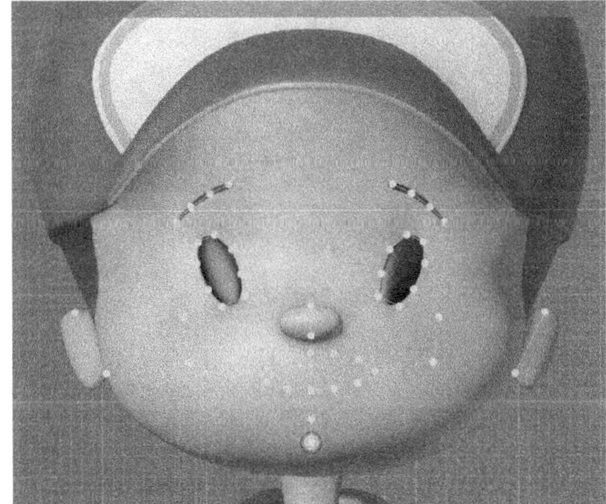

This toolbox is a very cost-effective add-on product, which is deeply loved by users, so it occupies the Blender Market rankings all year round.

The animation function of this paid add-on is basically the same as the free built-in Rigify add-on, which generates a rig with controllers for 3D characters and then animates them by manipulating the controllers, which you can consider it as an enhanced version of Rigify.

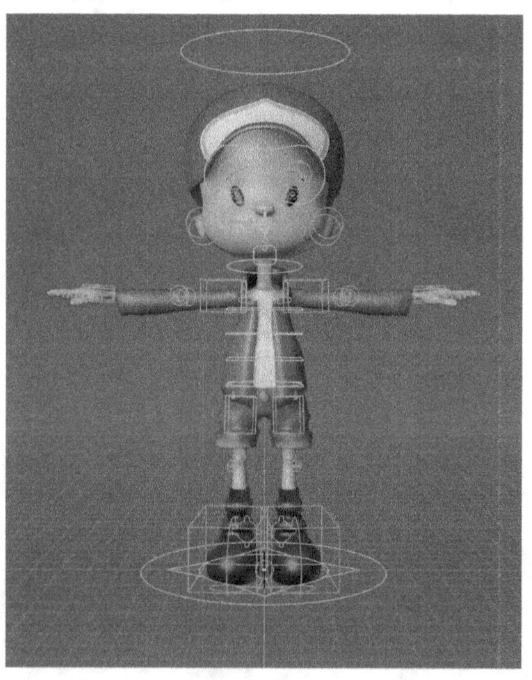

I personally think the biggest feature of this add-on is the semi-automatic alignment of the skeleton, which can save you a lot of time when binding the skeleton for 3D characters. The principle of its semi-automatic alignment is to manually place some marker points in the front view, and then the add-on will simulate the emission of light towards the screen to detect the depth distance of the marker points, so as to achieve the three-dimensional positioning of the marker points. The most technical positioning algorithm of this add-on is the finger positioning algorithm, which is automatically detected by the point cloud based contour generation algorithm, generating a more accurate spatial location of the finger joints, basically without manual adjustment.

Another highlight of this add-on is that it can export FBX files for game engines, saving users money by not having to purchase other paid FBX add-ons separately.

The add-on costs $40, with free lifetime upgrades after purchase. Recommended for professional Unity or Unreal independent developers and small teams to buy to improve animation production efficiency.

## What is Motion Capture Technology?

Motion capture technology, that is, the real person wearing a marked costume with multiple cameras to capture the movement of the real person's limbs and expressions, or inertial sensors to capture the movement of the real person's limbs and expressions, and then transfer the movement to the 3D character, so that the 3D character performs the same action and expressions as the real person.

Motion capture technology is widely used in film and animation, and the famous 3D movie "Avatar" was realized with optical motion capture technology.

Whether it is to buy high-precision optical motion capture kit wearing with markers of motion capture clothing, or to buy inertial sensor-based design of motion capture kit, for independent developers and small teams with limited budgets are a bit difficult.

So cheap solutions based on deep learning came into being, such as Google's MediaPipe project, which uses an ordinary camera to get facial expressions and body skeleton tracking in real time. Someone based on MediaPipe SDK, developed an add-on for motion capture - "BlendArMocap", which is free and open source on Github (https:// github.com/cgtinker/BlendArMocap), it is possible to achieve expression and motion capture directly through the computer camera in Blender.

Of course, the result of the cheap solution is not comparable to that of the professional solution, but basically, it can be used to create simple animations, such as walking, running, jumping, etc. These common movements can be correctly recognized by the deep learning algorithm, but some strange poses may not be recognized, and the animation will be a mess, while the optical motion capture-based solution or sensor-based motion capture solution, even the strangest poses have no problem and can be recognized very well.

## Purchase Motion Capture Animations from Major Resource Stores

In addition to purchasing your own motion capture equipment and asking actors to perform actions to achieve motion capture, you can also purchase ready-made motion libraries from major resource stores for your own 3D characters.

## What is Animation Retargeting Technique?

Animation retargeting technique is to transfer the animation of one kind of 3D character to another kind of 3D character, for example, you can transfer the animation of 3D humanoid character to anthropomorphic 3D animal character, and let the anthropomorphic 3D animal character perform the same action as 3D humanoid character. Animation retargeting technique can achieve the reuse of animation data, which can avoid making the same animation repeatedly.

## Retarget Motion Capture Animation to Character

With motion capture animation data, we can use animation retargeting technology to transfer captured skeletal animation and expression animation to 3D characters, including characters, animals, and even anthropomorphic cars, so that 3D characters can perform the same actions and expressions as real people.

If you want to use ready-made add-ons for animation retargeting, I recommend two free and open source add-ons - "Blender Retarget" (https://github.com/igelbox/blender-retarget) and "Expy Kit" (https://github.com/pKrime/Expy-Kit).

The "Blender Retarget" add-on uses "Driver" instead of "Constraint" to implement animation retargeting, using Python code to calculate the correct pose and update the bones in real time, which has the advantage of not adding additional constraints to the bones.

The "Blender Retarget" add-on also has the function of automatic bone mapping, which is unique in its implementation principle.

Instead of using bone names matching, the two rigs are matched according to their spatial positions, and if the two rigs have very similar poses and are placed in overlapping positions, the mapping results will be very accurate and only a few incorrect bone mappings need to be manually adjusted.

The "Blender Retarget" add-on also has disadvantages, because the priority of "Driver" is lower than the priority of "Constraint", it can only do animation retargeting for simple rigs that do not use constraints, but not for complex rigs like Rigify that use controllers.

While the "Expy Kit" add-on uses "Constraint" other than "Driver" to implement animation retargeting from "Mixamo" skeleton animations, "Unreal Engine" skeleton animations, "Rigify" meta-rig animations, "Rigify" deform rig animations, "Rigify" controller animations, "Render People" skeleton animations, and "Daz Genesis 8" skeleton animations retargeted to Rigify rig.

The automatic bone mapping of the "Expy Kit" add-on is achieved by hard-coded bone names, which is very convenient for the above popular rigs to do animation retargeting, but there is almost no way to use customized rigs because the "Expy Kit" add-on cannot recognize the bone names in customized rigs.

The "Expy Kit" add-on is implemented by first generating a Rigify meta-rig with identical dimensions from the source rig, and then automatically generating a rig with controllers using Rigify's own functions. Then, the "Copy Rotation" constraints and "Copy Location" constraints are added to the Rigify deform rig, and the source rig is used to drive the Rigify deform rig. It can also bake animations to Rigify controllers, which is very powerful.

Note that when using this add-on, it is best to change the "Limb Segments" of the thighs and arms in the meta-rig from the default value of 2 to 1 before generating the rig with controllers. This is because the add-on will only add constraints to the first limb bone when doing animation retargeting, the second limb bone will be ignored. If you use the default value to generate two limbs, you need to manually add a "Copy Rotation" constraint for the second limb, with "Target" set to the source rig and "Bone" set to the first limb bone for the retargeting animation to be correct.

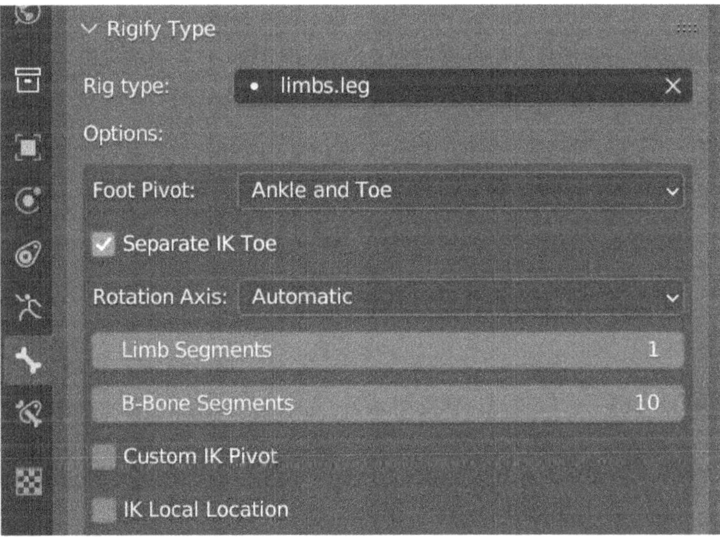


There are always various problems with ready-made add-ons, and if you know how animation retargeting works, you will know how to solve these unexpected problems.

I have used many animation retargeting add-ons, but none of them can perfectly solve the animation retargeting problem, which is caused by the complexity of the rig. The rig is composed of deform bones, IK bones, drivers, controllers, and various constraints, like a large and complex manipulation equipment. This complexity leads to a variety of problems when retargeting animations.

In order to solve the animation retargeting problem completely, we need to analyze the skeleton-driven mechanism in Blender to get the perfect solution.

Blender's deform bones are the most useful bones, they are like the bones that are actually attached to the body of the 3D character, they are the ones that actually drive the animation of the 3D character. The other bones are auxiliary bones that provide convenience for the user to manipulate the rig.

If we retarget the animation directly to the deform bones, there are two methods - The first method is to use "Driver", which can encapsulate the bone mapping algorithm into a function and calculate it in real time through Python code; the second method is to use "Constraint", which copies the action of the source bone to the target bone by adding various constraints to the deform bone.

If a bone has "Driver" and "Constraint" simultaneous, because "Constraint" has a higher priority than "Driver", it makes "Driver" inactive and blocked by "Constraint".

So if you want to achieve animation retargeting for bones with "Constraint", you can remove the "Constraint" from the bones first, and then do the animation retargeting, it will be much easier.

The specific approach is to generate a simple rig without constraints from a complex rig, and then do animation retargeting for this simple rig. This workflow is only suitable for game development, but because of the extra step of generating another rig, it seems a bit redundant if you don't do game development.

If I want to do animation retargeting directly on a complex rig, how to achieve it? After a thorough research, I found a robust method to do animation retargeting directly on complex rigs. This method only requires to add the "Copy Rotation" constraint on all the deform bones to achieve a copy of the bone rotation; then add the "Copy Location" constraint on all the root bones to achieve a copy of the root bone position; if you also need IK positioning of the hands and feet, you can add IK "Constraints" for the hands and feet and constrain them to the target object.

Here we take the complex Rigify rig and explain the process of doing the animation retargeting purely by hand.

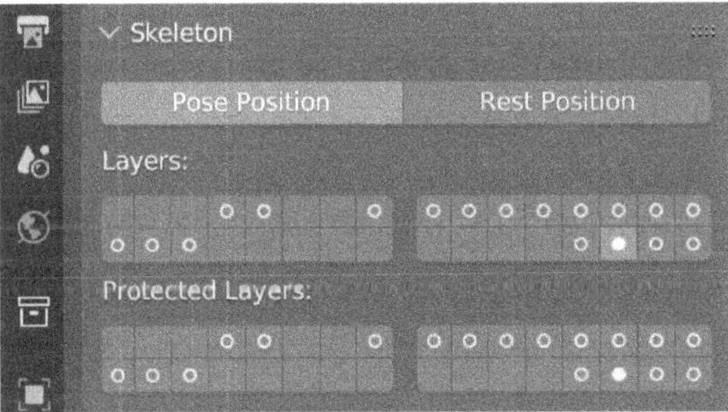

Rigify rig hides the "deform bones" layer by default, click the "Skeleton" tab in the "Properties" window, find the "Skeleton"

section, click the third-to-last layer of the "Pose Position" layer, deform bones layer will be displayed.

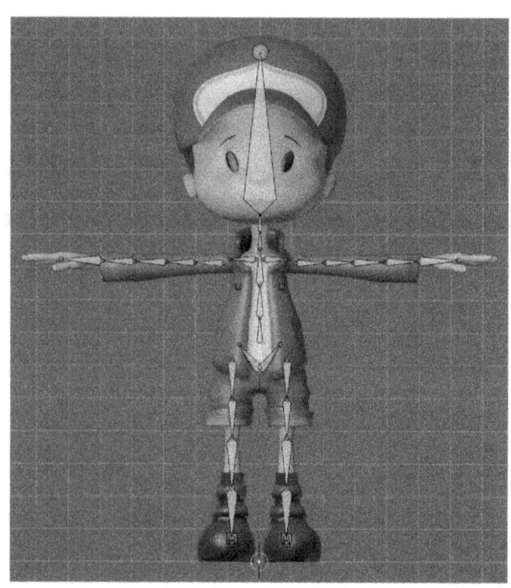

Once the deform bones layer is displayed, click on the rig in the "3D View", press the "Ctrl + Tab" key to switch to "POSE" mode, and add a "Copy Rotation" constraint to each deform bones, with "Target" set to the source rig, and "Bone" set to the corresponding bone on the source rig.

By adding the "Copy Rotation" constraint, the rotation direction of both bones will immediately become identical, and when the bones in the source rig rotate, the deform bones in the target rig will also rotate with them.

What if the initial orientation of the source bone and that of the target bone are not the same? The solution is simple - Just add a child bone to the source bone, adjust its initial orientation so that its initial orientation is almost identical to that of the target bone, and then constrain the target bone to this newly added child bone.

If you play the animation, you will find that the retargeted animation just animates in place, with the two arms, two shoulders, two thighs and the torso losing the up-and-down undulating motion of the root bone. This is because multiple deform bone chains in Rigify are not connected to each other, but rely on other auxiliary bones to connect into a complete rig, which results in multiple deform bone chains not being able to transfer their positions to each other.

So we also need to retarget the position information of the bones to the root bones of the deform bone chains, and add another "Copy Location" constraint for the two arms, two shoulders, two thighs and the torso, with "Target" set to the source rig and "Bone" set to the corresponding bone on the source rig. If you play the animation, you will find that the retargeted animation is not only in place, but also the two arms, two thighs and the torso have an up and down movement, which makes the retargeting animation complete.

If you find that the 3D character is walking slippery, you can add another IK constraint for the foot's deform bone to force it to the source rig's foot position; if the 3D character is holding a weapon in his hand, you can also add another IK constraint for the hand's deform bone to force it to the weapon's position.

Learning this purely manual workflow will solve almost all animation retargeting problems.

## Entrepreneurship Class

---

## Financing is a Double-Edged Sword

Nowadays, the most popular model for starting a business is to use a project plan to finance it.

But there is no free lunch, there are benefits and drawbacks of relying on financing to start a business. The first disadvantage is that sufficient funds will temporarily cover the entrepreneur's own ability and cover the defects of the profit model, the crisis will delay the outbreak. The second disadvantage is that, as the saying goes, "Gifts blind the eyes", after financing, the development direction of the company will certainly be influenced by investors, you have to become as eager as the capital, in a utilitarian mentality is not easy to make good products.

Although the growth rate of starting from scratch is slow, you can spend time slowly polishing best products, and in the process of groping, your business and your ability will improve simultaneously, thus being more resistant to risk, and the road ahead will be more robust.

You can examine the fact that many entrepreneurs who started with nothing can do so for decades, while most of the nouveau riche entrepreneurs who rise by external financing do not last more than three to five years.

In this book, I mainly talk about how to start a business without external financing, because this is the actual situation of the majority of independent developers and small teams, they have no way to pull in financing, generally rely on parental funding or personal savings as start-up capital to start their business, if they can rely on the right perception of entrepreneurial to success, it will be more universal significance.

## Technology Threshold + Niche Product + Timely Assistance = Success

When starting a business, don't do what is popular in the market, because the popular projects in the market are generally very competitive and require sufficient funds and industry experience to stand firm, so it is not recommended for independent developers and small teams to start a business when they rashly choose a popular project, either funds or industry experience are not advantageous.

As independent developers and small teams, the easiest product to succeed in starting a business is to make a product with a technical barrier, of niche, filling a gap in the market, and one that really helps others solve their problems. As long as you can make such a product, find and sell it to your target customer base, you'll be successful, it's that simple.

First of all, a good product for independent developers and small teams should have certain technical barriers. Otherwise, if your product is just made and others see it, they will immediately invest much more money than you to make the same type of product to compete with you once they see that the product can make money and is easy to copy. As an independent developer or a small team, what advantage do you have to compete with the big companies? Therefore, it is easy to fail in business if you do not have technical barriers.

Second, a good product for independent developers and small teams should also be a niche product. The niche product mentioned here does not mean the number of users is small, but the volume of the product is small, you can calculate the volume of the product by multiplying the number of users of the product by the value of each user. Big companies are like lions, need to hunt big preys around in the grassland to survive, for very small prey, such as grasshoppers in the grass, simply ignore, because the lion spend energy to catch grasshoppers must be more than worth the loss. If you make product in the market is only equivalent to grasshoppers, big companies do not care to compete with you, or even if they have the intention to do will have to give up because the effort is greater than the harvest. Doing such a niche product, feeding independent developers and small teams is more than enough, you will naturally avoid a very large number of strong competitors.

Finally, a good product for independent developers and small teams should also be a gap in the market, can really help others to solve problems, I call such a product "Timely Assistant", that is to say, bring real help to your target users, make users pay for your product and at the mean time, they will appreciate that you have brought them such a useful product.

If you can't meet the above three conditions simultaneously, but independent developers and small teams with top-notch technology, you can also choose to make the "Icing on the Cake" type of product, that is to say, there are already similar products in the market, you think you can do better, you need to innovate on the basis of competing products and surpass them in order to gain a certain market. The advantage of making the "Icing on the Cake" type of product is that you don't have to spend energy to find the market gap, but directly choose to force the overtaking with super technical strength, because your opponent will also lower the price, and your opponent will also strengthen the publicity, so the only thing you can do is to use technology to overtake the opponent. But because you have lost the first opportunity in the market, if the opponent is not too stupid, to achieve a straight overtaking is of some difficulty, so the difficulty of making the "Icing on the Cake" products is greater than that of making the "Timely Assistant" products.

The most laborious and unpleasant practice is to do micro-innovation without any technical barriers, which is to copy other people's products. If a product can be easily copied, it means that its technical difficulty is not great, you can copy others', others can copy yours, you copy each other, the homogenization of products is serious, you can only rely on brand and money to compete, independent developers and small teams have neither a strong brand nor sufficient funds, which can easily lead to business failure.

To summarize: independent developers and small teams making technically demanding, niche market, timely assistant products are more likely to succeed.

## Which is Better, Mass Market or Niche Market?

On the Internet, marketplaces appear as platforms, such as Amazon, Apple App Store, Unity Asset Store, Unreal Marketplace, etc..

It is not practical for independent developers to build their own platform, and even if you have the technical ability to create one of your own, the results will not be good.

I have done experiments to sell the same software on two platforms simultaneously, the first one is my self-built platform through the FastSpring website, and the second one is Unity Asset Store, because the rental fee of the self-built platform is very low, I deliberately adjusted the price of the self-built platform to be lower than that of Unity Asset Store when I experimented, hoping that users would be better off shopping on my self-built platform so that I could get more of a cut. But the results were embarrassing, as more than 80% of the users still chose to buy software from the high-priced Unity Asset Store.

What is the reason for this? Later I figured out that the essence of business is trust, people are afraid to shop on untrusted platforms, preferring to shop on reliable and mature platforms, even if the price is more expensive.

If I choose an existing established platform, which is better to choose a big platform or a small one?

The big platform is like the sea, your product is like throwing a stone into the sea, the general product can only be found by search, if the search result is too far back, it can not be found by the user, the phenomenon of winner takes all is more obvious on the network platform. To open a physical store, you just have to do the best on the street; while on the network platform, you have to do the best on the whole platform.

If you want to put your product on a big platform, there are only three ways to win: the first way is to make the product excellent that editors will notice your product and put it on the list by the editors' manual recommendation, but each time it is selected will only last for about a week or two; the second way is to make the product good enough that when users search for keywords, the search result must be on the first page; the third way is to invest money in advertising so that your product appears frequently in the advertising space on the page, so that users can find your product. As far as I know, the advertising budget of long-term advertising is quite high, independent developers and small teams can hardly afford. If you can't achieve these three things, it's not recommended to choose a big platform.

Independent developers and small teams are better off choosing professional niche platforms to prevent your product from being drowned in the sea and to make it very easy for your target users to find your product.

After solving the problem of product exposure, if your product is good enough, you can usually get a high paid conversion rate and thus a significant income.

# Chapter 5 Character Export

## Import and Export Characters with Blender's Free Built-in FBX Add-on

The format of FBX is a closed-source format of AutoDesk, which is not publicly available, but some hackers have successfully analyzed the binary format of certain versions of FBX by reverse engineering.

Blender's built-in free FBX import/export add-on is based precisely on the hacked version of the FBX format, and although it can import and export FBX files, it is not perfect. For example, it can only import certain versions of binary format of FBX files, and FBX files in text format cannot be imported; the exported FBX files are not optimized for game engines, when importing into game engines, the scales of the armature and the models aren't 1.0, which may lead to wrong animation retargeting result.

If you only want to exchange files with 3ds Max or Maya, Blender's free built-in FBX import/export add-on is still usable. But if you need to export FBX files for game engines, I don't recommend it.

If you need to export FBX files to major game engines, it is recommended that you purchase the "Better FBX Importer & Exporter" add-on from the "Blender Market" website (also by me), which is based on the official AutoDesk FBX SDK and designed specifically for the game development workflow. It solves the above problems in Blender's free built-in FBX add-on.

## Export Characters for Godot Engine with the Free Customized Collada Add-on

Although Blender has a built-in Collada import and export feature, Godot Engine has officially rewritten a Collada add-on for Blender with better compatibility, specifically for exporting 3D character models and animations from Blender to Godot Engine in DAE format. If you use Godot Engine to develop games, Godot Engine's official Collada add-on is the best choice.

## Import and Export Characters with the Paid "Better FBX Importer & Exporter" Add-on

To solve the problems in Blender's free built-in FBX add-on, I wrote the "Better FBX Importer & Exporter" add-on for Blender in 2019, which is based on the official AutoDesk FBX SDK, with the goal of providing a better compatibility for Blender's game development workflow.

Blender uses the famous GPL license, which requires that any tightly integrated add-on must also use a GPL-compatible license, so Blender cannot directly integrate with AutoDesk's closed-source FBX SDK, but the GPL license allows interaction with other closed-source softwares that are not based on the GPL license through simple system calls, this is not in conflict with the open source idea, otherwise, if the GPL license does not allow interaction to any other closed-source softwares, it would really be a cocoon.

I designed this FBX add-on by dividing the add-on into two parts: a GPL part and a non-GPL part, and invented an efficient and elegant

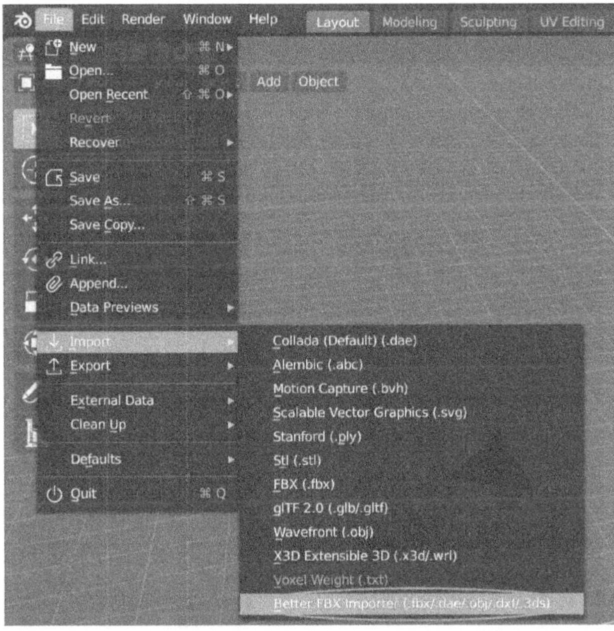

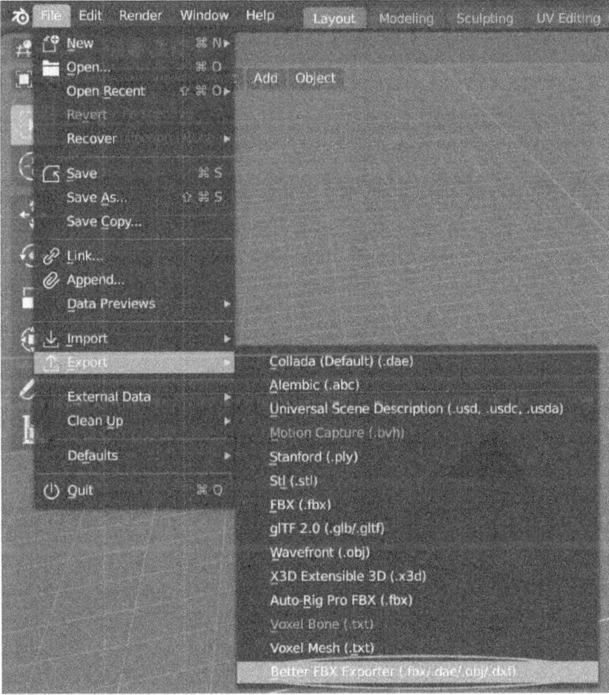

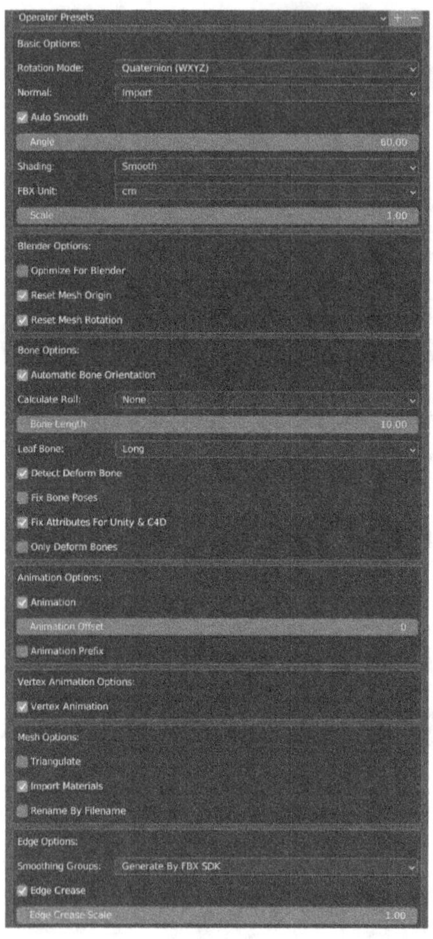

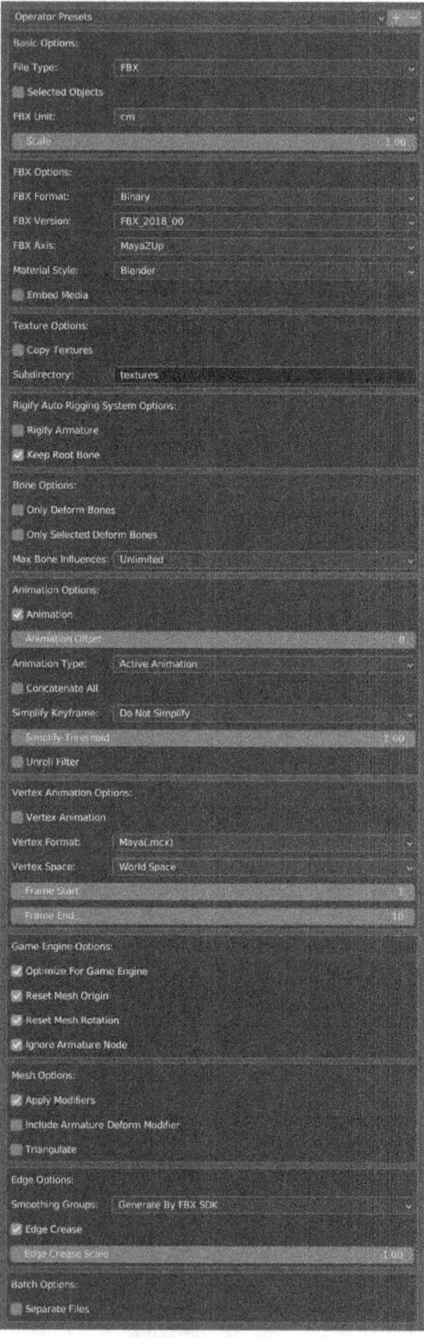

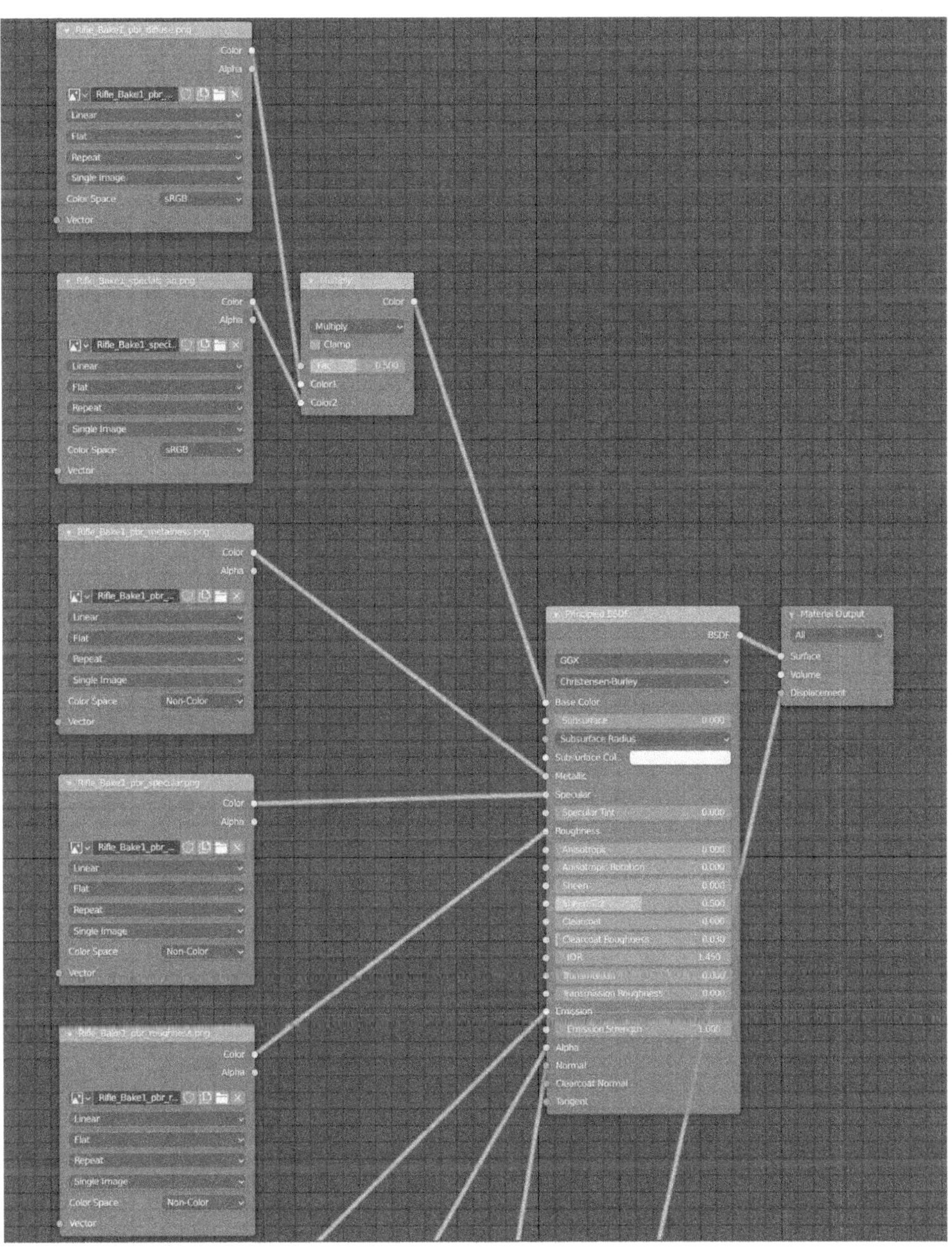

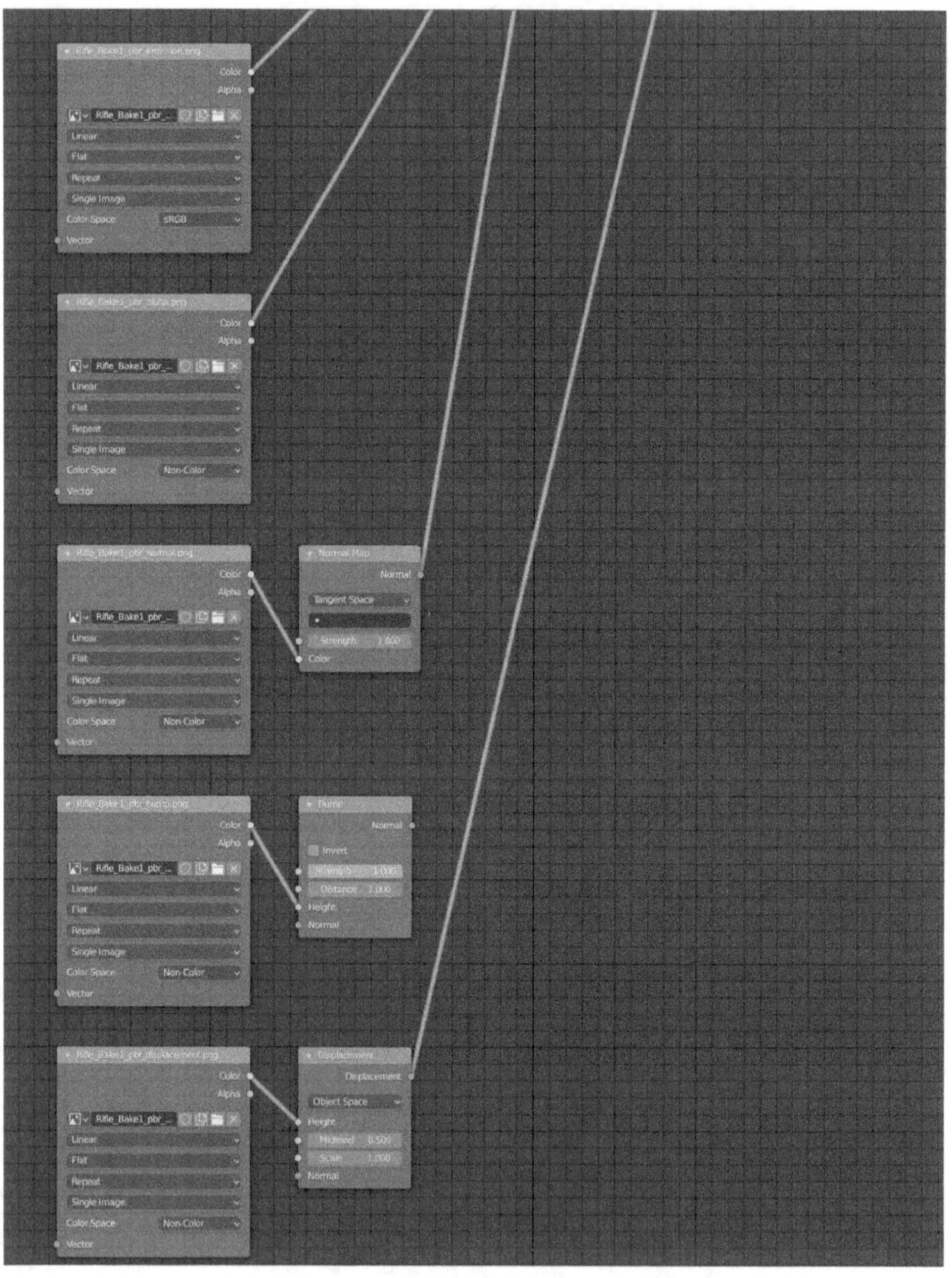

intermediate data format to isolate the GPL part from the non-GPL part. the GPL part only interacts with the intermediate data format, and the non-GPL part also only interacts with the intermediate data format. When the add-on works, the GPL part interacts with the non-GPL part through a simple system call, thus resolving the conflict between the open source and closed-source licenses.

This add-on focuses on the game development workflow and can import files in FBX, DAE, OBJ, DXF and 3DS formats and export files in FBX, DAE, OBJ and DXF formats.

This add-on automatically adjusts the orientation of all bones by default when importing skeleton, and can guarantee the correctness of the imported animations. It solves the problem caused by different bones orientations in different 3D softwares, no matter what bones orientation is used for the original skeleton, after importing into Blender, it can guarantee that the bones orientation and the imported animations are correct in Blender.

This add-on supports exporting 9 channels of PBR materials, Unity Engine can recognize 4 PBR channels; Unreal Engine can recognize 6 PBR channels, after importing into Unity Engine and Unreal Engine, the recognized PBR channels will be automatically setup successfully.

PBR channels that can be exported by Blender:

Base Color

Ambient Occlusion

Metallic

Specular

Roughness

Emission

Alpha

Normal

Displacement

PBR channels that can be automatically imported by Unity Engine:

Albedo

Metallic

Roughness

Normal Map

PBR channels that can be automatically imported by Unreal Engine:

Basic Color

Metallic

Specular

Roughness

Emissive Color

Normal

When exporting PBR textures, only static textures are supported, you need to bake the procedure textures with other baking add-ons, such as the free and open source "EasyPBRBake" (https://

github.com/meshonline/EasyPBRBake), or go to Blender Market to buy paid PBR baking add-ons, such as "SimpleBake" (https://www.blendermarket.com/products/simplebake---simple-pbr-and-other-baking-in-blender-2), which can bake procedure textures to static textures with one click. After manually replacing the procedure textures with the static textures, you can export the PBR material with this add-on.

This add-on uses game engine friendly parameters by default when exporting, ensuring that the scales of skeletons and meshes are 1.0 in game engines, and animations can be retargeted correctly in game engines.

This add-on also supports exporting generic Rigify animations, not only for 3D humanoid characters, but also for bipedal animals, such as birds; for quadrupeds, such as horses and wolves; and for sea creatures, such as sharks; and even for strange creatures such as one-legged monsters and three-headed monsters that you created by yourself.

The exported Rigify animations support any game engines, including Unity Engine, Unreal Engine, Godot Engine, and even your own game engine.

If you use Rigify to make animations, it will be very convenient to export animations with this add-on. About how to export Rigify animation with this add-on, there is a detailed video tutorial on the product page, due to the length limitation, I won't repeat it here.

This add-on was designed specifically for the game development workflow and has made an important contribution to helping Blender get out of the island of game development.

You can buy this add-on at Blender Market for $28, once you have purchased the add-on, you will automatically receive free lifetime upgrades and one-on-one technical support for any technical problems you encounter, such as fixing bugs, requesting for new features and answering questions about the add-on, etc..

The best investment in the world is to make an investment in your own education. With the guidance of a master, a novice can make progress much faster.

The parameters in the importer:

Rotation Mode

You can chooce your favorite rotation mode.

The default parameter is 'Quaternion (WXYZ)'.

Normal

'Calculate' means that we don't use imported normals, we let Blender generate normals for us.

'Import' means that we use imported normals.

The default parameter is 'Import'.

Auto Smooth

Auto smooth (based on smooth/sharp faces/edges and angle between faces).

The default parameter is enabled.

Angle

Maximum angle between face normals that will be considered as smooth.

The default parameter is 60.0 degrees.

Shading

How to render and display faces.

'Smooth' means that render and display faces smooth, using interpolated vertex normals.

'Flat' means that render and display faces uniform, using face normals.

The default parameter is 'Smooth'.

FBX Unit

You can choose your favorite FBX unit from 'mm', 'dm', 'cm', 'm', 'km', 'Inch', 'Foot', 'Mile', and 'Yard'.

The default parameter is 'cm'.

Scale

If the imported 3D model looks too small or too large, you may change the value to let it have proper size.

The default parameter is 1.0.

Optimize For Blender

When enabled, make Blender friendly rotation and scale.

When disabled, keep original rotation and scale.

The default parameter is disabled.

Reset Mesh Origin

When enabled, reset mesh origin to zero when 'Optimize For Blender' is enabled.

When disabled, keep mesh origin when 'Optimize For Blender' is enabled.

The default parameter is enabled.

Reset Mesh Rotation

When enabled, reset mesh rotation to zero when 'Optimize For Blender' is enabled.

When disabled, keep mesh rotation when 'Optimize For Blender' is enabled.

The default parameter is enabled.

Automatic Bone Orientation

Automatically sort bones orientations, if you want to preserve the original armature, please disable the option.

The default parameter is enabled.

Calculate Roll

Automatically fix alignment of imported bones' axes when 'Automatic Bone Orientation' is enabled.

The default parameter is 'None'.

Bone Length

Bone length when 'Automatic Bone Orientation' is disabled.

The default parameter is 10.0.

Leaf Bone

There are two leaf bone styles - 'Long' and 'Short'.

'Long' means that the length of a leaf bone is equal to 1/1 of the length of its parent bone.

'Short' means that the length of a leaf bone is equal to 1/10 of the length of its parent bone.

The 'Long' style lets you easily select leaf bones, the 'Short' style make the armature looks more beautiful.

The default parameter is 'Long'.

Detect Deform Bone

When enabled, detect and setup deform bones automatically.

When disabled, does not detect and setup deform bones automatically.

The default parameter is enabled.

Note: If you are importing a pure armature which is not skinned by any meshes, please disable the option, otherwise, all bones will be wrongly setup as non-deform bones.

Fix Bone Poses

When enabled, try fixing bone poses with default poses whenever bind poses are not equal to default poses.

When disabled, does not try fixing bone poses with default poses whenever bind poses are not equal to default poses.

The default parameter is disabled.

Fix Attributes For Unity & C4D

When enabled, try fixing null attributes for Unity's FBX exporter & C4D's FBX exporter, but it may bring extra fake bones.

When disabled, nodes without any attributes will be ignored.

The default parameter is enabled.

Only Deform Bones

When enabled, imports only deform bones.

When disabled, imports all bones, include IK bones, deform bones, and control bones.

The default parameter is disabled.

Animation

When enabled, imports the armature, the animation action and shape key action.

When disabled, only imports the armature with bind pose and blend shapes.

The default parameter is enabled.

Animation Offset

Add an offset to all keyframes.

The default parameter is 0.

Animation Prefix

When enabled, add object name as animation prefix.

When disabled, does not add object name as animation prefix.

The default parameter is disabled.

Vertex Animation

When enabled, imports vertex animation.

When disabled, does not import vertex animation.

The default parameter is enabled.

Triangulate

When enabled, converts polygon to triangle.

When disabled, does not convert polygon to triangle.

The default parameter is disabled.

Import Materials

When enabled, import materials for meshes.

When disabled, does not import materials for meshes.

The default parameter is enabled.

Rename By Filename

When enabled, rename imported meshes or armatures by their filenames, it only works when importing multiple files.

When disabled, does not rename imported meshes or armatures with their filenames, it only works when importing multiple files.

The default parameter is disabled.

Smoothing Groups

How to generate smoothing groups.

The default parameter is 'Generate By FBX SDK'.

Edge Crease

When enabled, imports edge crease weights.

When disabled, does not import edge crease weights.

The default parameter is enabled.

Edge Crease Scale

Scale of edge crease weights.

The default parameter is 1.0.

The parameters in the exporter:

File Type

You can choose FBX, DAE, OBJ or DXF to export.

The default parameter is 'FBX'.

Selected Objects

When enabled, exports selected objects on visible layers.

When disabled, exports all objects in the scene.

The default parameter is disabled.

FBX Unit

You can choose your favorite FBX unit from 'mm', 'dm', 'cm', 'm', 'km', 'Inch', 'Foot', 'Mile', and 'Yard'.

The default parameter is 'cm'.

Scale

If the exported 3D model looks too small or too large, you may change the value to let it have proper size.

The default parameter is 1.0.

FBX Format

You can choose your favorite FBX format.

The default parameter is 'Binary'.

FBX Version

You can choose your favorite FBX version.

The default parameter is 'FBX_2018_00'.

FBX Axis

You can choose your favorite FBX Axis from 'MayaZUp', 'OpenGL', 'Unity', 'Unreal1', 'Unreal2'.

The default parameter is 'MayaZUp'.

Material Style

You can choose your favorite material style.

The default parameter is 'Blender'.

Embed Media

When enabled, embed all texture images into FBX file.

When disabled, does not embed any texture images into FBX file.

The default parameter is disabled.

Copy Textures

When enabled, if not embed media, copy texture images to user-defined subdirectory.

When disabled, does not copy texture images to user-defined subdirectory.

The default parameter is disabled.

Subdirectory

User-defined subdirectory in the same directory of the exported file.

The default parameter is "textures".

Note: If you use an empty string, the exporter will copy all the texture files into the same directory of the exported file.

Rigify Armature

When enabled, exports game-friendly armature for Rigify Auto-Rigging System.

When disabled, exports generic armature.

The default parameter is disabled.

Keep Root Bone

When enabled, keep the root bone when making game-friendly armature for Rigify Auto-Rigging System.

When disabled, does not keep the root bone when making game-friendly armature for Rigify Auto-Rigging System.

The default parameter is enabled.

Only Deform Bones

When enabled, exports only deform bones.

When disabled, exports all bones, include IK bones, deform bones, and control bones.

The default parameter is disabled.

Only Selected Deform Bones

When enabled, exports only selected deform bones in 'EDIT' mode.

When disabled, exports all deform bones.

The default parameter is disabled.

Max Bone Influences

Maximum bone influences you can have per vertex.

2: Suitable for mobile game.

3: Suitable for mobile game.

4: Suitable for mobile game.

6: Suitable for desktop game.

8: Suitable for desktop game.

Unlimited: Suitable for generic animation.

The default parameter is Unlimited.

Animation

When enabled, exports the armature, the animation action and shape key action.

When disabled, only exports the armature with bind pose and blend shapes.

The default parameter is enabled.

Animation Offset

Add an offset to all keyframes.

The default parameter is 0.

Animation Type

You can choose to export active animation, all actions, or all NLA tracks.

The default parameter is 'Active Animation'.

Concatenate All

When enabled, concatenates all actions or all NLA tracks into a single action if 'Animation Type' is not 'Active Animation'.

When disabled, exports separate actions or separate NLA tracks if 'Animation Type' is not 'Active Animation'.

The default parameter is disabled.

Simplify Keyframe

You can choose from multiple keyframe simplification algorithms to simplify keyframes.

The default parameter is 'Do Not Simplify'.

Simplify Keyframe Factor

How much to simplify keyframe values (0.0 to disable, the higher the more simplified).

The default parameter is 1.0.

Unroll Filter

When enabled, fix unexpected sudden rolls.

When disabled, does not fix unexpected sudden rolls.

The default parameter is disabled.

Vertex Animation

When enabled, exports vertex animation.

When disabled, does not export vertex animation.

The default parameter is disabled.

Vertex Format

You can choose 'Maya(.mcx)' or '3ds Max(.pc2)' to export.

The default parameter is 'Maya(.mcx)'.

Vertex Space

You can choose 'Local Space' or 'World Space'.

The default parameter is 'World Space'.

Frame Start

The start frame of vertex animation.

The default parameter is 1.

Frame End

The end frame of vertex animation.

The default parameter is 10.

Optimize For Game Engine

When enabled, make game engine friendly rotation and scale.

When disabled, keep original rotation and scale.

The default parameter is enabled.

Reset Mesh Origin

When enabled, reset mesh origin to zero when 'Optimize For Game Engine' is enabled.

When disabled, keep mesh origin when 'Optimize For Game Engine' is enabled.

The default parameter is enabled.

Reset Mesh Rotation

When enabled, reset mesh rotation to zero when 'Optimize For Game Engine' is enabled.

When disabled, keep mesh rotation when 'Optimize For Game Engine' is enabled.

The default parameter is enabled.

Ignore Armature Node

When enabled, does not export the armature node as a dummy node.

When disabled, exports the armature node as a dummy node.

The default parameter is enabled.

Apply Modifiers

When enabled, apply all modifiers on mesh objects except armature deform ones, but all mesh objects with shape keys will be ignored.

When disabled, does not apply all modifiers on mesh objects.

The default parameter is enabled.

 Include Armature Deform Modifier

When enabled, apply armature deform modifiers on mesh objects too when the 'Apply Modifiers' option is enabled.

When disabled, does not apply armature deform modifiers on mesh objects.

The default parameter is disabled.

Triangulate

When enabled, converts polygon to triangle.

When disabled, does not convert polygon to triangle.

The default parameter is disabled.

Smoothing Groups

How to generate smoothing groups.

The default parameter is 'Generate By FBX SDK'.

Edge Crease

When enabled, exports edge crease weights.

When disabled, does not export edge crease weights.

The default parameter is enabled.

Edge Crease Scale

Scale of edge crease weights.

The default parameter is 1.0.

Separate Files

When enabled, exports to separate files by object name.

When disabled, exports to a single file.

The default parameter is disabled.

## Entrepreneurship Class

---

## Genuine Software and Business Password

Only when you use genuine products, you can understand how the genuine users think, know why users should pay for software, and realize the business password that belongs to you only. If you don't even want to spend money on software yourself, how can you expect others to spend money on your software?

I don't know if you've heard of the saying "Moral Bank", which says that everyone has a moral bank in which they store not money but their blessings. If you lose something, you will gain something, and if you gain something, you lose something. When a person does bad things, they are consuming their blessings; when a person does good things, they are accumulating their blessings. When a person has consumed his blessings, his good fortune comes to an end.

So what is the ultimate business password? One's wealth is the result of one's accumulated blessings. If one accumulates more blessings, one exchanges more, and if one accumulates less blessings, one exchanges less.

Honest management, accumulating virtues and doing good deeds are the foundation of a century-old enterprise.

How many people still believe these "clichés" today? Blessed are those who believe.

## Deeply Cultivate an Area of Expertise

If you have made many products, you will find that more than eighty percent of your revenue comes from only one product, and the revenue from other products is just a fraction.

But it is not that other products are not important, if all your products belong to the same field and accumulate slowly, they can provide users with a complete set of solutions.

What I mean is that we ordinary people do not make products with a hammer in the east and a stick in the west, it is best to plow deep in a field in order to achieve a cumulative effect and achieve value enhancement.

If you are an entrepreneurial genius, you can also try multiple fields. There are always exceptions to everything, and for a few talented entrepreneurs, it's not absolute whether you want to plunge deep into one field.

## Argue with Yourself

Developers are usually lack of objective evaluation of their own products.

You are so passionate about your product that you feel like you are changing the world with it. In your imagination, when your product comes out across the world, there will be lightning and thunder, and then there will be sunshine, and the world will change for this.

To be able to know your product objectively, you can try to describe your product to your family members, preferably someone who know nothing about it, and then listen to their ideas.

There is another way - play a naive guy in your mind, ask yourself all kinds of naive and childish questions, and argue with yourself; when you are discouraged by the naive and childish guy's questions, then play back to the wise you and explain to the naive and childish guy how good your product is.

With this approach of playing two persons for brainstorming, you can maintain the passion of entrepreneurship as well as identify the flaws of your product so that you can objectively evaluate your product.

The book was written in such a way, outsiders can always see the problem.

# Chapter 6 Import Character into Major Game Engines

## How to Import Character into Unity Engine?

If you are using Blender's built-in FBX add-on, there may be problems with the exported scaling. Since the scaling is not 1.0, it may cause problems with animation retargeting, and some PBR texture channels need to be set manually.

If you are using the "Better FBX Importer & Exporter" add-on, by default, the add-on exports game engine friendly armature and models with a scale of 1.0, and there will be no problems with animation retargeting in game engines; when exporting, set the

material type parameter to "Unity Engine", almost all PBR texture channels will be set successfully when importing into Unity Engine.

If you used "Embed Media" when exporting FBX, when importing into Unity Engine, first make sure the "Material Creation Mode" is "Import via MaterialDescription", click the "Extract Textures..." button to release the embedded textures, and the textures will be displayed properly.

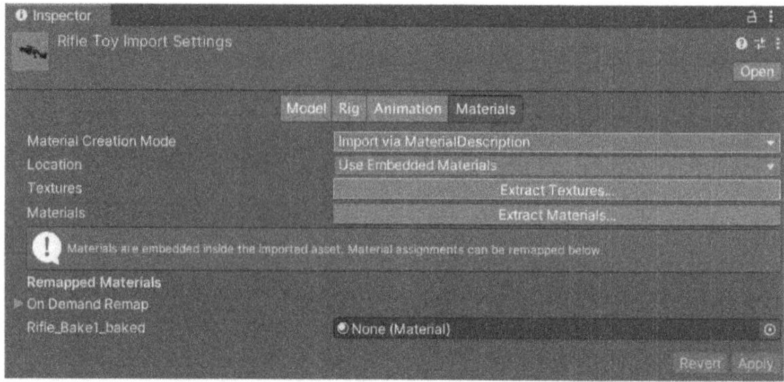

If you do not use "Embed Media" when exporting FBX, you need to drag the textures and model together into the "Unity Editor" Explorer window, or drag the textures into the "Unity Editor" Explorer window first, and then drag the model into the "Unity Editor" Explorer window. The order is important, add the textures first and then the model, otherwise the "Unity Editor" will not find the textures for the model and the textures will not show up. When importing into Unity Engine, make sure the "Material Creation Mode" is "Import via MaterialDescription" and click "Extract Materials..." button to release the embedded materials, and the materials will be displayed properly.

After importing the Rigify character into Unity Engine, if you need to do animation retargeting, you can change the "Rig -> Animation Type" from "Generic" to "Humanoid", and you don't need to change anything, the animation retargeting will be successful.

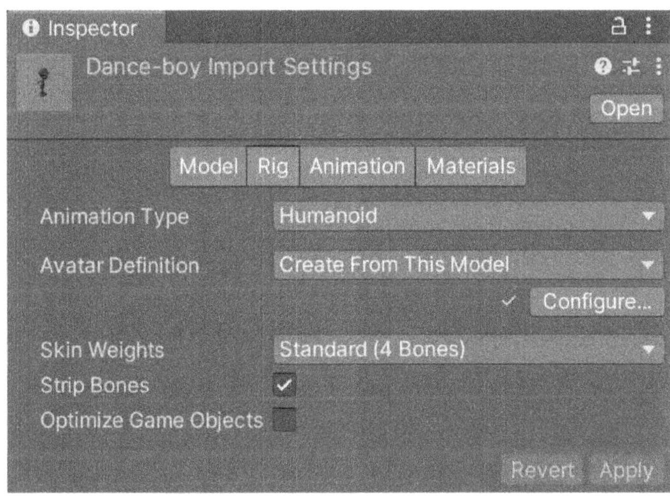

## How to Import Character into Unreal Engine?

If you are using Blender's built-in FBX add-on, there may be problems with the exported scaling. Since the scaling is not 1.0, it may cause problems with animation retargeting, and some PBR texture channels need to be set manually.

If you are using the "Better FBX Importer & Exporter" add-on, by default, the add-on exports game engine friendly armature and models with a scale of 1.0, and there will be no problems with animation retargeting in game engines; when exporting, set the material type parameter to "Unreal Engine", almost all PBR texture channels will be set successfully when importing into Unreal Engine.

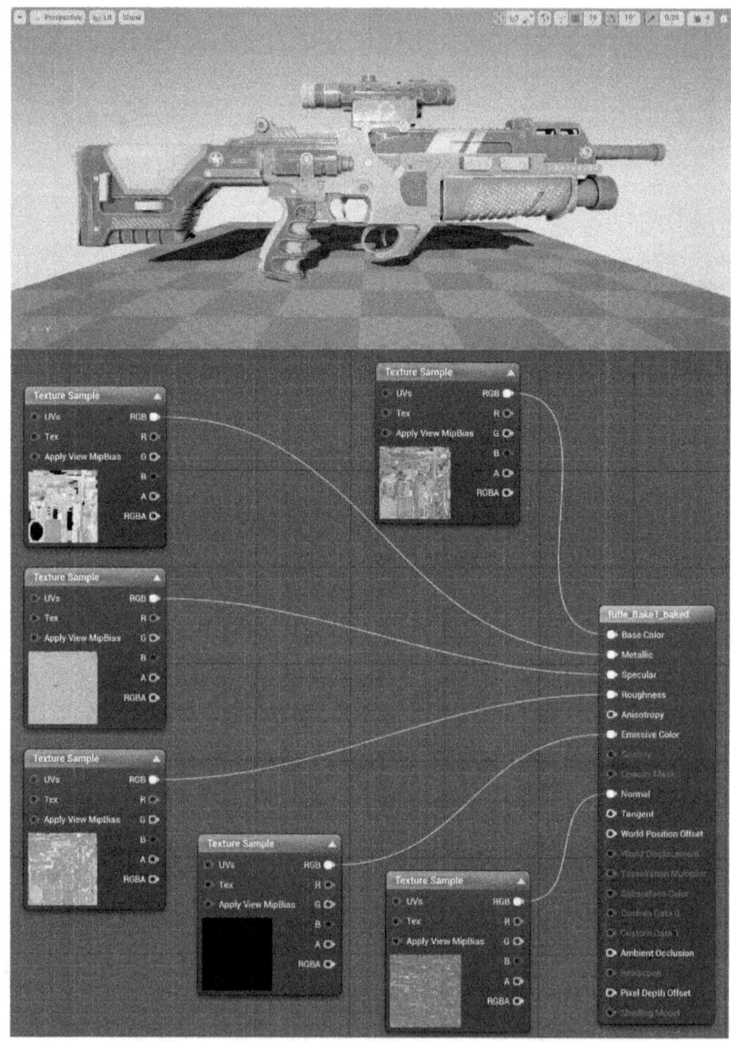

After importing the Rigify character into Unreal Engine, if you need to do animation retargeting, double click the imported skeleton to automatically open the "Skeleton Editor", click the menu "Window

-> Retarget Manager" to display the "Retargeting Manager" tab, click the "Select Rig" drop-down box, select "Select Humanoid Rig", then click "AutoMap" button for automatic bones mapping. Most of the bones are mapped to the correct bones, but a small number of bones are mapped to the wrong bones and need to be corrected manually.

After fixing the bones mapping, click on the "Skeleton Tree" tab, right click on the root bone, select "Recursively Set Translation Retargeting Skeleton" in the popup menu, all the bones are set to "Skeleton" type, then set the "root" bone to "Animation" type, set the "DEF-spine" bone to "Animation Scaled" type.

Click the "Save" button in the upper left corner to save the settings and close the "Skeleton Editor". In Unreal Engine's "Resource Management" window, find a certain animation file that can be used for retargeting, right-click it, and select "Retarget Anim Assets -> Duplicate Anim Assets and Retarget" from the pop-up menu. Select the skeleton to be retargeted, click the "Retarget" button, and a new retargeted animation will be automatically generated for the skeleton.

## How to Import Character into Godot Engine?

Godot Engine is an open source software, officially recommends the Collada format, and offers a free customized version of the Collada add-on for exporting Collada files from Blender.

Because Collada does not have a unified code implementation library, the compatibility of Collada format from different manufacturers is not very good; while FBX SDK has only one official implementation, although it is a monopoly and the code is closed-source, but because of the high degree of unified compatibility, FBX has become a de facto industry standard instead, and is more widely used than Collada.

Since it is a free add-on officially provided by Godot Engine, I recommend users to prefer using it to export 3D characters to Godot Engine.

The Better "FBX Importer & Exporter" add-on does not only export FBX files, but also export Collada characters models to Godot Engine.

If you find that the character model exported by the Godot Engine's official Collada add-on have issues, you can also try this add-on, and maybe you can solve the problem.

## How to Import Character into Your Own Game Engine?

Importing characters into your own engine is a big challenge. Because both FBX format and Collada format are designed for exchanging data between 3D softwares, not optimally designed for game engines, the loading speed is generally slow.

What I did back then was to use the FBX SDK to parse the FBX file, write the data needed by my own game engine to a custom compact binary format file, and load the compact binary format file when the game engine loads the data, which would be very fast.

If you don't have a need for data confidentiality and loading speed, in addition to parsing FBX files with the FBX SDK, you can use the intermediate format exported by the "Better FBX Importer & Exporter" add-on as input to your own engine.

Because I was inspired by the context-independent syntax of compiler design theory when I designed this intermediate format, every line in the file is context-independent.

This context-independent syntax greatly simplifies the design of syntax parsers, which can be implemented with very concise code.

The add-on provides the full Python source code for the syntax parser, which you can easily port to C++ or other languages for importing data into your own engine.

However, the intermediate format I designed is a plain text format that humans can easily read and understand, no data confidentiality at all and the parsing speed is much slower than that of the binary FBX.

If you need data confidentiality or need to maximize the parsing speed and the loading speed, I still recommend you to use AutoDesk's official FBX SDK to parse FBX files and generate engine specific binary format files to import into your own engine for use.

The FBX SDK contains a sample project called "ImportScene" with full source code. This project implemented the entire process of traversing the FBX file, and if you want to export data to your own engine, you can do so by inserting your own code into each traversal function. It is easy to understand the meaning of the data because each traversal function will parse the data before displaying it on the screen. If you want to write the data to a file, it is very easy to implement.

Another programming resource you can refer to for the FBX SDK is Unreal Engine. After installing Unreal Engine, it will install the source code of some plugins, including the source code of the FBX import and export plugin. When you encounter difficulties and can't implement it, you can check its source code and learn how it is implemented, and maybe your problems can be solved.

Importing into your own engine is an advanced topic that involves FBX SDK programming, so this book will not discuss the detailed steps, but only present some possible implementation ideas and provide some programming resources. I believe that this information is enough for a real master.

## Entrepreneurship Class

---

## The Trap of Small Teams - Capital Chain Rupture

After a small team starts a business with their own savings or receives angel investment, they are excited to rent an office, buy equipment, hire employees and prepare for a big job.

A rupture of capital chain is always the biggest risk for small teams, and it is even more serious than for independent developers and big companies. Because independent developers can scrimp and save to last longer; big companies can subsidize losing projects with other profitable projects.

Why? Because product maturity is a cycle, you must spend a very long time to polish and iterate your product to be accepted by the end user, and only by the end user is considered successful. Just like hatching a chick, it takes twenty-one days for an egg to become a chick, so it's useless to rush. As a small team, you have to persist until that day.

Spending other people's money generally does not hurt, but when the money runs out, your business is over. As a small team, you should cut down on all unnecessary expenses. For example, register a virtual address and work from home to save money on renting an office; the biggest cost of a software company is the salary, so you should save money during the start-up period, for example, the co-founders only pay the basic living expenses. In short, don't burn money, leave enough time for experimentation and growth, and stick to the day when the product is mature.

## The Narrow Escape Venture Capital Model

The most popular entrepreneurial model today is the venture capital model.

Simply put, suddenly one day, you have a great idea in your mind, so you are so excited that you write a project plan without sleeping for three days and nights, and go to big cities to find investors.

The investor has so much money that he worries about how to spend his money, and he is also looking for a project that can make a lot of money, so he picks up your project plan and looks at it. "Wow! It really looks amazing. I will invest in this project !", so you get the first round of angel investment.

Although it seems to have infinite scenery on the surface, there is a lot of money to spend at the beginning of the business, this entrepreneurship model is really a narrow escape game, anyway, I will not touch the venture capital model, I would rather start from scratch.

The success of a project is determined by the ability and profitability model of the entrepreneur. The huge amount of cash can cover up the lack of ability and the defect of the profitability model, and finally the crisis will be concentrated and lead to the failure of the venture.

When you have a lot of money, if you are starting a business for the first time, both the ability and experience are certainly not enough and need to be worked out in dealing with various problems. But sufficient cash will cover up the problems, the ability is not improved, and finally when the problems are concentrated, you are at a loss.

When you have more money, you will ignore the most essential profit model problems, thinking that you can rely on more money to win in the market competition, and finally found that more money can not solve the fundamental problem of profit model.

When you have a lot of money, but also because it is to spend other people's money, so spend money generously will not hurt, commonly known as burning money, however, if the project does not take off when the money is almost burnt out, there is a high probability that the next round of investment will not be available and the project will fail due to the capital chain rupture.

When you have a lot of money, even if the project is going well and can get multiple rounds of investment, the future development process of the project will be held hostage by the capital, you can't control your own project in the future development. Investors are usually in a hurry, to get listed for cash is their ultimate goal, and do not care about the project's future. Due to the lack of decision-making power, you may watch your project go in the wrong direction and not be able to do anything about it.

Business failed, wasted youth is also cost-effective, after a few failed business ventures, you find yourself no longer young. Business failure will also combat your confidence, you may think that you are not suitable for entrepreneurship, from then on find a job to fool around, or just lie down and pose.

If you can follow the right entrepreneurial thinking, starting with small projects, work steadily, slowly accumulate experience, improve your ability, and accumulate more funds, you can then do a large project can be managed. In other words, you could have started a successful business, but prematurely killed by venture capital.

If you really want to support your family by starting a successful business, it is not recommended to choose the venture capital model.

## Products! Products! Still Products!

You may have mastered a skill through this book, and you will be faced with a major choice at this point - Is it to put in a resume and get an offer, is it to stay at home and take on outsourcing online? Or do you want to make products to sell in the resource store?

If you put in a resume to get an offer, it is still the same as using time for money, paying for one day to get paid for one day, only 30 days per month, not much room for growth.

Taking on outsourcing online is better than putting in a resume and getting an offer. As you take on more outsourcing, your experience grows and you get more and more outsourcing. But the trouble with outsourcing is that you have to redo every task, even if it's based on previous project modifications, which means that there is a time cost to replicate the outsourced tasks. Even if you receive a lot of outsourcing tasks, you can't work 24 hours a day, right? There is a limit to the number of outsourcing tasks that can be completed.

My advice is to make a product, because once you make a product, your earnings are completely proportional to the sales of the product, for example, if the unit price of the product is ten dollars, if you sell one hundred copies, you can get a thousand dollars of earnings; if you sell one hundred thousand copies, you can get a million dollars of earnings. The no-cost replicability of the product is a guarantee of entrepreneurial success.

So, if you really want to start a business, making products is the best choice. You may say, "Of course I know it's good to make a product, but it's not that easy to make a product."

Making products is not as difficult as you might think, and I have grouped innovation into two categories.

1. Vertical innovation that expands in depth.

2. Horizontal innovation that expands in breadth.

If you are talented, you can focus on innovation in depth and do technically difficult projects to form a technical barrier so that the chasers cannot surpass you.

If you are not so talented, you can focus on innovation in breadth and increase the competitiveness of your product by increasing the volume without increasing the price.

For example, assuming you've mastered 3D modeling, if you made a nice 3D model of an African elephant and put it in the TurboSquid model store, priced it for sale at $35, you might find that your sales would probably be dismal.

Why? $35 is not a low price even in the US, but it's not a high price either, it's a normal price that individual users can afford. Maybe someone who happens to need an African elephant model will pay $35 for your African elephant model; but for a more general application scenario, the user needs more than one African animal model, maybe he also needs other African animal models, such as lion, giraffe, and African buffalo, etc.. If each animal model costs $35 to purchase, the total cost will be very high and will greatly exceed the user's project budget, and that's where the problem is.

How to increase sales? By the price war promotions that domestic merchants are good at? I find it interesting that in the US markets, price reductions have little help to increase sales. In other words, at a price point that is already not too high, price cuts have little effect on increasing sales volume. The US users are concerned about value for money, and a ridiculously low price may instead make the US users think that the quality of your product is definitely not high, and turn to other competing products. As the unit price decreases, while the number of sales does not increase almost, sales will decline instead.

There is a better product strategy to achieve a win-win situation for both users and businesses. In the business world, a tried and tested product strategy is called "Increase the quantity but not the price", digital products are not replicated cost, since a single animal model is not attractive to users, you can make a whole set of 3D models of

African animals and sell them in the form of product bundle, and sell them for $35, or even higher, for example, $70.

You will find that sales of the product bundle will increase substantially. What if others make bundle too? You can bind skeleton for all animal models, generate level of details, and even create skeletal animations for all animal models, turning them into game-ready resources that will make users see your products and have an impulse of "Buying is to earn!"

That's what I mean by horizontal innovation, which is not very technical, but so feature-rich that it's irresistible. When others feel that your product is value for money, your product will be a big hit. If you can generalize, the above ideas can be extended to any products.

After the above analysis, you will find that compared with one-to-one outsourcing on the Internet, or spend a lot of energy to learn and proficient in a variety of complex 3D softwares, and then go to a big company to put in a resume to get offer also underpaid by HR to enjoy the 996 blessings, but to make a product is the easiest thing. Ordinary people can also make successful products.

## Go Your Own Way, Steady is the Best

Let's say, entrepreneurship is like you are rowing a small boat sailing on the sea, you are the captain, the way to reach the other side varies, each person can choose a different method according to his/her own characteristics. Some people like to take risks, with a project plan to find investment everywhere, make a big bet; some people like to play it safe, step by step.

I myself like the steady method, the feeling of repeated failure is not good, need strong psychological quality to withstand the blow of business failure; waste of youth is also cost-effective. Yesterday also splurged, today can not afford to buy noodles, such days are a bit like the days of gamblers, anyway, I don't like it.

Starting a business ought to be successful, if you can rely on a business you like to support your family, but also do not have to worry about the 35-year-old career crisis, in your spare time, you can do whatever you want, just thinking about it will make you feel happy.

In my more than twenty years of independent development, I have never lost money on any of my projects, it is only a matter of making more or less money. My strategy is to only do projects with a high success rate, build up slowly and grow steadily, and this entrepreneurial feeling is really good.

It is said that there are only two kinds of animals that can climb up to the top of the pyramid - eagles and snails. Most of us are ordinary people, can not be a soaring eagle, but does not mean that ordinary people are not worthy of entrepreneurship, for ordinary entrepreneurs, to be a slow moving happy snail, but is the best choice.

# Download 3D Character for Tutorial from the Mixamo Website

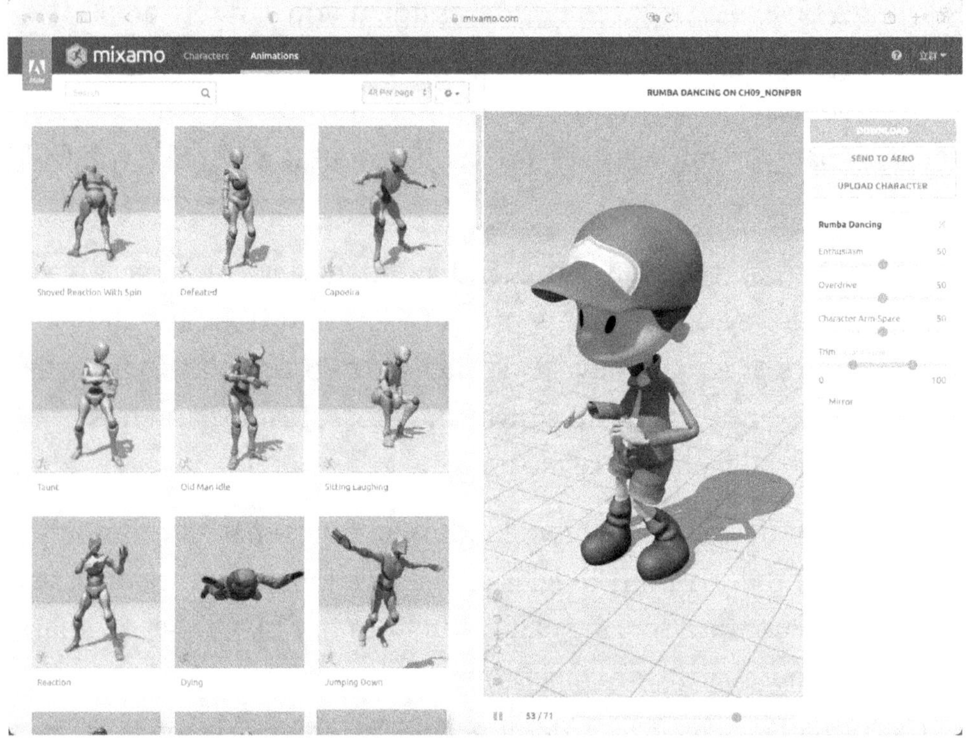

First, we go to the Mixamo website (https://www.mixamo.com/) to download a 3D character for tutorial purpose.

You need an Adobe account, if you don't have yet, you need to register one, after logging into your account, click on the "Characters" tab, find and click on the "Timmy" character; click on the "Animations" tab, find and click on the "Rumba Dancing" animation. Wait a moment, in the right 3D view, the cartoon boy Timmy will keep dancing rumba in a loop.

Click the "Download" button in the upper right corner of the page to bring up the "Download Settings" interface. The default setting is to download the 3D character in FBX format with animation, which is exactly what we need. Click on the "Download" button at the bottom right corner of the "Download Settings" interface. It will prompt you to wait a few moments and the download will begin shortly. Once downloaded locally, the filename will be "Rumba Dancing.fbx".

## Hands-on Tutorial on How to Bind Character with Rigify

We'll start our Rigify tutorial with the cartoon character we just downloaded, assuming you have enabled the "Rigify" add-on in Blender and have installed the "Better FBX Importer & Exporter" add-on.

First start Blender, press the "A" key in the "3D View" to select all objects in the scene, then press the "X" key, a small window will pop up next to the mouse to confirm the deletion, click "Delete", all objects in the scene will be deleted immediately.

Click the menu "File -> Import -> Better FBX Importer", in the pop-up interface of the add-on parameters, change the "Leaf Bone" from " Long" to "Short", this is to make the end bones shorter, thus look better, click the "Better Import FBX" button to import the character model.

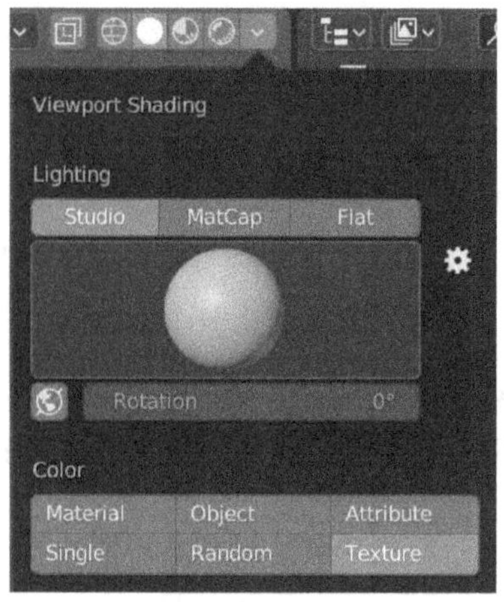

Blender just started does not display textures by default, only the colors of the materials, so the 3D character's whole body is displayed as white, we need to switch to texture mode, click the down arrow icon to the right of several spherical icons in the upper right corner of the "3D View", it will show the current mode settings, click the "Texture" item under the "Color" section, you will find that the cartoon boy appears color on his body.

Click the "Skeleton" icon on the right side of the "Properties" window, expand the "Viewport Display" section, check the checkbox in front of "In Front", the armature will not be obscured by the body, always displayed in front.

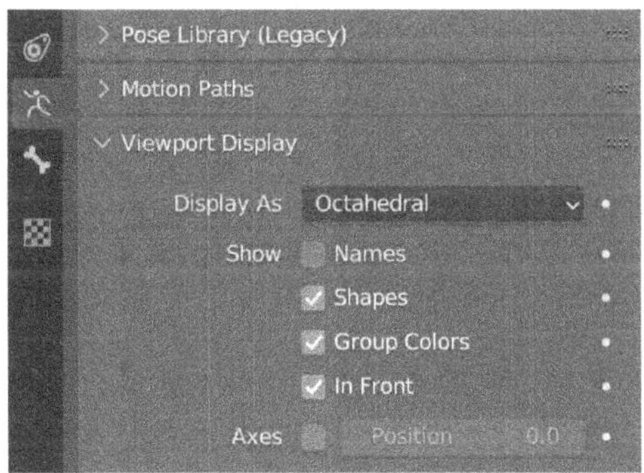

Drag the "Rotate", "Zoom" and "Pan" view controller on the right side of the "3D View" with the mouse to make the cartoon boy face the screen at the right size. Press the "Spacebar" key in the "3D View" and the cartoon boy starts animating. Since the cartoon boy's animation is only 72 frames long, and Blender starts with a default animation frame range of frame 1 to frame 250, frames 73 to 250 are stationary. Click on "End" in the "Timeline" window below, type 72 and press enter, the animation will loop between frame 1 and frame 72. Press the "ESC" key in the "3D View" to end the animation.

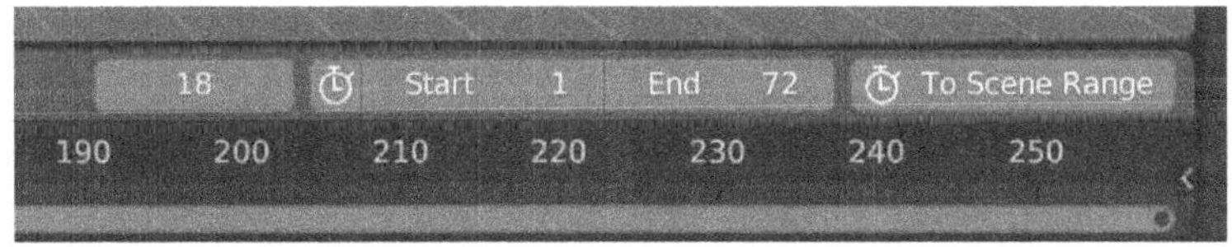

Here's what we're going to do, separate the cartoon boy from the armature as we bind it to the brand new Rigify rig.

The units in FBX are centimeters (cm), while the units in Blender are meters (m), a difference of 100 times. When importing the FBX file, the armature is virtually shrunk by a factor of 100, while the actual skeleton size and the actual model size are still 100 times the Blender default units.

We can do this by clicking on the character model, pressing the "Alt + P" key in the "3D View", and selecting "Clear and Keep Transformation" in the pop-up menu. But the pose remains the same as in the animation.

We then click the wrench-shaped icon in the "Properties" window on the right, switch to the "Modifier" window and find that the pose is retained because the "Armature" modifier has not been removed, click the "X" button to the right of the "Armature" modifier, you will find that the character becomes a "T" pose.

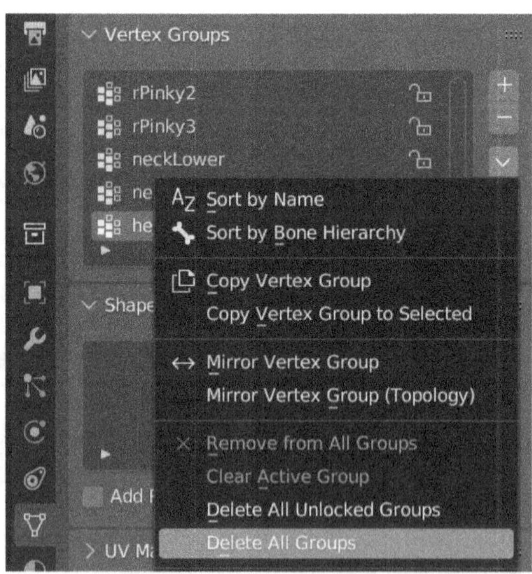

We click the green inverted triangle icon in the "Properties" window on the right, we will find that in the "Vertex Groups", there is still residual skinning information, click the down arrow on the right and select "Delete All Groups". and the remaining skinning information is deleted.

Finally, press the "Ctrl + A" key in the "3D View" and select "All Transforms", which will "apply" the translation, rotation and scaling. You can think of the "Apply" operation as writing the translation, rotation and scaling of the model as the vertex position inside the model, so that from the outside of the model, the model is at the origin, rotated to 0 and scaled to 1. The "Apply" operation is very important before doing binding and making animation in Blender.

After separating the character, the old armature is not really useful anymore, but instead of rushing to delete it, we hide it first, because it will still be useful when we do the animation retargeting in the next section, where we will retarget the animation to the brand new Rigify rig.

To hide the armature, you can click the small icon shaped like an eye on the armature item in the upper right corner of the outline view, or you can click the armature in the "3D View" and press the "H" key, both methods work.

After hiding the armature, only the cartoon boy is left in the scene. Let's start adding a Rigify rig.

In the "3D View", press the "Shift + A" key, and from the pop-up menu, select "Armature -> Basic -> Basic Human (Meta-Rig)", a basic human meta-rig will be added to the scene.

You will notice that the newly added meta-rig is much taller than the cartoon boy, and the skeleton is obscured by the character's body.

Click the "Skeleton" icon in the "Properties" window on the right, expand "Viewport Display", and click the checkbox in front of "In Front" to make the meta-rig always appear at the top.

We need to shrink the meta-rig to about the same size as the character, press the "S" key in the "3D View" to enter the zoom mode, move the mouse, the skeleton will zoom in or out as the mouse moves. When the two shoulder bones of the meta-rig are as high as the character's shoulders, click the left mouse button to end the "Scale" mode. Finally, in the "3D View", press the "Ctrl + A" key and select "Scale", this operation will "apply" the scaling of the meta skeleton, so that the meta-rig is scaled to 1.

Next, we need to enter "EDIT" mode to manually adjust the positions of the bones. In the "3D View", press the "Tab" key to enter "EDIT" mode, because our model and rig are symmetrical, we first press the "X" icon in the upper right corner to enter the "Mirror Operation" mode, so that when we adjust the position of one side of the rig, the other side of the rig will also follow.

This simple base meta-rig has no facial bones or finger bones, so it is easy to manually adjust the position of these meta-rig to align with the character's body with a little more time.

You can click the pan icon with four small arrows on the left toolbar to enter the "Pan" mode. After clicking a bone, a pan controller will appear around it, and you can move the bone by dragging the handle with the mouse.

It is more efficient to use the mouse to cooperate with shortcut keys, after selecting the bone, press the "G" key to enter the "Pan" mode, move the mouse, and then click the left mouse button to end the "Pan" mode after reaching the right position.

Adjusting the bone position requires viewing from multiple perspectives, you can click on the letters of the axes on the "View Rotation" controller (X, Y, Z, +X, +Y, +Z, -X, -Y, -Z) to quickly switch to different orthogonal views. If you are used to adjusting the position of the bones in perspective, you can also freely rotate the view to observe the position of the bones from various angles.

If you need to adjust the facial and finger bones in a more complex rig in the future, you can make good use of the "Snapping" feature. Click on the magnet-shaped icon at the top of the "3D View" to enable the "Snapping" feature, and click on the down arrow next to it to select the snapping type, which includes "By vertices", "By edges", "By faces", and "By volume". In the process of adjusting the position of the bones, the bones will be snapped to the closest vertex, edge, face, or volume, which can greatly speed up the alignment of the bones.

After adjusting all the bone positions, press the "Tab" key again to exit "EDIT" mode.

Click on the skeleton icon in the "Properties" window on the right, scroll the mouse wheel and click on the "Generate Rig" button under the "Rigify" section, and the magic happens.

At this point the meta-rig is useless and can be deleted, but it is better to hide it first, in case you need to adjust the position of the meta-rig again in the future or need to add new bones, you can regenerate the rig with controllers from the meta-rig.

Click to select the newly generated rig with controllers, click the "Skeleton" icon in the "Properties" window on the right, expand "Viewport Display", and click the checkbox in front of "In Front" to make the rig with controllers always displayed at the top.

The last step is to bind the cartoon boy to the rig with controllers. The easiest way to achieve this is to use Blender's built-in surface heat diffuse skinning algorithm, in the "3D View", click to select the character model, then hold down the "Shift" key and click to select the rig with controllers, press the "Ctrl + P "key, select "Armature Deform - With Automatic Weights" in the pop-up menu, wait for a few seconds, the skinning is complete.

Here we test the skinning results, in the "3D View", click on the rig with controllers, press the "Ctrl + Tab" key to enter "POSE" mode, try to move the red-colored IK controller, the body will move with the controller and make the corresponding movement, the skinning result is good. After testing, press the "Ctrl + Tab" key again to exit "POSE" mode.

If you also have the "Voxel Heat Diffuse Skinning" add-on installed, you can also try the voxel skinning again.

Click on the character model in the "3D View", then click on the rig with controllers. The voxel skinning add-on does not require the order of selection, either one can be chosen first.

Press the "N" key in the "3D View", the hidden right sidebar will be shown, click the "Mesh Online" tab, click the "Voxel Heat Diffuse Skinning" button, the add-on will report the progress in light blue text, wait a moment and the skinning will be finished.

Going into "POSE" mode again to test the skinning results, for this cartoon boy model, both skinning methods yield good results. But for more complex models, such as character models with many accessories of clothes and equipment, the two-stage skinning method of the voxel skinning add-on generates better skinning results.

## Hands-on Tutorial on How to Retarget Animation to Rigify Character

As an exercise, we do the animation retargeting purely by hand, a method that can handle any complex rigs.

Recall from Chapter 4 that the secret to purely manually animation retargeting is to add a child bone to the source bone that has the exact same initial orientation as the target bone, and then constrain the target bone to the corresponding child bone. Because of the large number of bones, creating child bones with the exact same initial orientation as all the target bones is cumbersome. If we can make a copy of all the target bones, merge them into the source rig, and make them child bones of the corresponding source bones by adjusting the parent-child relationship of the bones, we can speed up this process.

Click on the rig with controllers, press the "Shift + D" key in the "3D View" and press the "Enter" key, this will duplicate an identical rig out.

To make it easier to see and manipulate the rig when merging it, we need to hide the controllers of the rig we just duplicated, and only show the original shapes of the bones. Click the rig you just duplicated, click the "Skeleton" tab in the "Properties" window on the right, find the "Viewport Display" section, click the small triangle next to it to expand it, you can see that the "Shapes" item is enabled by default, which means that if the bone has a controller, only the controller of the bone will be displayed, hiding the original shape of the bone. Click the checkbox in front of "Shapes" to disable it, so that the bone does not show the controller, but only the original bone shape.

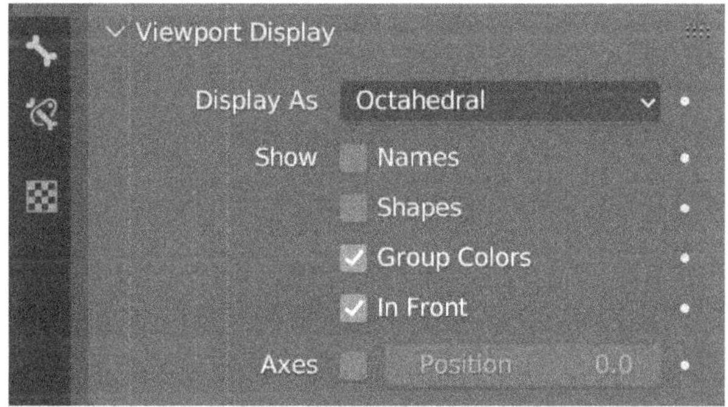

In the next step we remove all the bones other than the FK bones. Since the bones are distributed in multiple layers, we will first show all the layers. Click on the rig you just duplicated, click on the "Skeleton" tab in the "Properties" window on the right, find the "Skeleton" section, hold down the "Shift" key and click on all the layers in the "Pose Position" layer, bones in all the layers will be displayed.

How to quickly find all the bones except FK bones from so many bones? There is a visual bones classification chart in the right sidebar, we can hide all the FK bones by this visual bones classification chart, then the remaining bones are all other bones except the FK bones. Press the "N" key in the "3D View" to display the right sidebar, switch to the "Item" tab, expand the "Rig Layers" section, and you can see that the bones classification chart. By default, all the bone types are displayed, click "Torso", "Arm.L(FK)", "Arm.R(FK)", "Leg.L(FK)", and "Leg.R(FK)", we have hidden all the FK bones. In the "3D View", press the "Tab" key to enter "EDIT" mode, press the "A" key to select all the unhidden bones, press the "X" key, and in the pop-up window, click "Delete" in the pop-up window, all the unhidden bones will be deleted, press the "Tab" key again to exit "EDIT" mode. Click "Torso", "Arm.L(FK)", "Arm.R(FK)", "Leg.L(FK)", and "Leg.R(FK)", all FK bones are redisplayed, and the rig will contain only FK bones.

Before merging the rig, there is one more problem to solve, we need to clean up the residual constraint information on the FK bones, otherwise, it will cause unpredictable interference to the animation retargeting. In the "3D View", press the "Ctrl + Tab" key to enter "POSE" mode, press the "A" key to select all the FK bones, select menu "Pose -> Constraints -> Clear Pose Constraints", all the constraints on the FK bones will be cleared. Press the "Ctrl + Tab" key again to exit "POSE" mode.

Now we can merge the two rigs into one rig. Click in the "3D View" to select the rig you just duplicated, then hold down the "Shift" key and click to select the source rig, the order of clicking is very important, then press the "Ctrl + J" key, the duplicated rig will be merged into the source rig.

We find that the newly merged FK bones have disappeared, this is because the source rig only shows the first layer by default, while the merged FK bones are in other layers, we need to show all layers. Click on the source rig, click on the "Skeleton" tab in the "Properties" window on the right, find the "Skeleton" section, hold down the "Shift" key and click on all the layers in the "Pose Position" tab, and all the bones in all layers will be displayed.

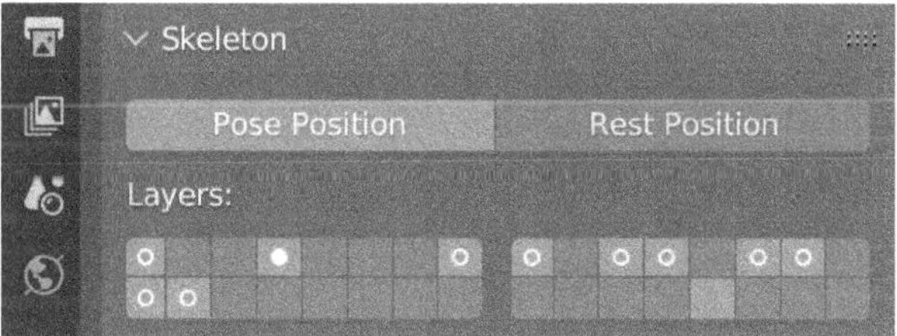

The next task is to adjust the parent-child relationship of the bones, so that the merged FK bones become the children of the corresponding source bones. In the "3D View", press the "Tab" key to enter "EDIT" mode, click to select a new merged bone, then hold down the "Shift" key and click to select the corresponding source bone, press the "Ctrl + P" key, select "Keep Offset" in the pop-up menu, and the new merged bone will become a child bone of the selected source bone. Repeat the above steps until all the new bones become child bones of the corresponding source bones, and press the "Tab" key again to exit "EDIT" mode.

If you press the "Spacebar" key to play the animation, you will see that all the merged FK bones follow the movement of the source bones. If you find that some bones are not following, it means it was forgotten and you need to go back and re-add it as a child bone of the corresponding source bone.

The next task is to add constraints to the bone so that the target bone exactly replicates the action of the source bone. Since the bones classification chart shows all bone types by default, we need to hide all bones other than the FK bones for ease of operation. In the "3D View", click the rig with controllers, and in the "Rig Layers"

section of the "Item" tab in the right sidebar, click "Torso(Tweak)", "Arm.L(IK)", "Arm.R(IK)", "Arm.L(Tweak)", "Arm.R(Tweak)", "Leg.L(IK)", "Leg.R(IK)", "Leg.L(Tweak)", "Leg.R(Tweak)", and "Root", hide all IK bones and Tweak bones, and show only FK bones.

We first add a "Copy Rotation" constraint to every FK bone to achieve an exact copy of the rotation action. Click on the rig with controllers in the "3D View", press the "Ctrl + Tab" key to switch to "POSE" mode, click on the "Constraints" tab in the "Properties" window on the right, and add a "Copy Rotation" constraint to every FK bone. Set "Target" to the source rig, and "Bone" to a child bone with the exact same name on the source rig. Press the "Ctrl + Tab" key to exit "POSE" mode.

Bones with only the "Copy Rotation" constraint can only be animated in place, just like the torso pinned to a wall, and cannot move up and down, so we need to add another "Copy Location" constraint for the root bone, so that the whole rig can follow the up and down motion of the root bone. Click on the rig with controllers in the "3D View", press the "Ctrl + Tab" key to switch to "POSE" mode, click on the "Constraints" tab in the "Properties" window on the right, and add a "Copy Location" constraint for the "torso" bone, "Target" is set to the source rig, and "Bone" is set to a child bone with the exact same name on the source rig. Press the "Ctrl + Tab" key to exit "POSE" mode.

Press the "Spacebar" key to play animation and you will find that the cartoon boy's limbs look like they are held in place by ropes, only his torso is twisting, what's going on? This is because the Rigify add-on is working in IK mode by default, we need to switch to FK mode. Click on the rig with controllers, press the "Ctrl + Tab" key in the "3D View" to enter "POSE" mode, click to select any of the bones on a limb, such as the left forearm bone, in the "Item" tab of the right sidebar, find the "Rig Main Properties" section, drag the mouse to the right side of the "IK-FK" item to make the value 1.0, or click on the "IK-FK" item, enter "1" and press the "Enter" key. Repeat the above steps to switch all four limbs from IK mode to FK mode.

Press the "Spacebar" key to play animation, the animation is perfect.

## Hands-on Tutorial on How to Export Rigify Character

If you export the retargeted animation implemented by constraint directly, you will find that there is no animation data. Why is this? The reason is that there must be an "Action" in Blender's "Animation Manager" for the FBX add-on to think there is animation data to export. So we need to create an "Action" first.

Click on the rig with controllers, press the "Ctrl + Tab" key in the "3D View" to enter "POSE" mode, press the "A" key to select all the FK bones. Pull the timeline slider to frame 1, press the "I" key in the "3D View", and select "Location, Rotation & Scale" in the pop-up menu; pull the timeline slider to frame 72, press the "I" key, select "Location, Rotation & Scale" in the pop-up menu, press the "Ctrl + Tab" key again to exit "POSE"mode.

The above operation will generate an "Action" in the "Animation Manager" with a start frame of 1 and an end frame of 72.

Next, we export the FBX file with the "Better FBX Importer & Exporter" add-on.

In the "3D View" click to select the cartoon boy, then hold down the "Shift" key and click to select the rig with controllers, click on the menu "File -> Export -> Better FBX Exporter", click the checkbox in front of "Selected Objects", click the checkbox in front of "Embed Media", set "Material Style" to "Unity Engine", click the checkbox in front of "Rigify Armature", select a directory where you want to store the exported FBX file, and enter the filename "rigify-unity.fbx", click the "Better Export FBX" button, and you will export an FBX file with the name "rigify-unity.fbx" for Unity Engine.

Click again in the "3D View" to select the cartoon boy, then hold down the "Shift" key and click to select the rig with controllers, click on the menu "File -> Export -> Better FBX Exporter, click the checkbox in front of "Selected Objects", click the checkbox in front of "Embed Media", set "Material Style" to "Unreal Engine", click the checkbox in front of "Rigify Armature", select a directory where you want to store the exported FBX file, and enter the filename "rigify-unreal.fbx", click the "Better Export FBX" button, and you will export an FBX file with the name "rigify-unreal.fbx" for Unreal Engine.

## Hands-on Tutorial on How to Import Rigify Character into Unity Engine

Start the "Unity Editor", create a new directory in "Unity Explorer" and rename it to "Rigify".

Drag the exported "rigify-unity.fbx" into this directory and wait a moment for an icon to appear with a colorless cartoon boy image on top and a small triangle-shaped player like icon on the right, indicating that it contains animations.

Click on this icon, click on the "Materials" tab in the "Inspector" window on the right, click on the "Extract Textures..." button, a pop-up window will appear asking for the directory to release the textures, the default is the current directory, click "Choose", wait a moment, the textures will be released to the current directory, the cartoon boy in the icon shows the color.

We will also find another popup window in "Unity Editor" titled "NormalMap settings", indicating that a material is being used as a normal map and that the texture must be marked as a normal map in the import settings. Click the below "Fix now" button to let "Unity Editor" fix it automatically.

## Hands-on Tutorial on How to Retarget Animation to Rigify Character in Unity Engine

If you click on the "Rig" tab in the "Inspector" window on the right, you will see that the "Animation Type" is "Generic", which means that the animation type contained in the FBX file is a user-defined "normal" format, which can only be used for the corresponding skeleton in FBX.

If you drag the icon to the "Hierarchy" window to create an instance, then click on the small triangle-shaped player like icon to the right of the icon, drag the "rigAction" animation of the cyan triangle icon to the instance you just created, and click on the small triangle-shaped player button at the top of the scene, the cartoon boy will dance the rumba in the scene.

But the cartoon boy has his back to us, and the rumba stops after one dance. We need to change the value of the "Y" channel of "Rotation" from 0 to 180 in the "Inspector" window on the right, and then click on the icon of the cartoon boy in "Unity Explorer", click on the "Animation" tab in the "Inspector" window on the right, find the "Loop Time" item, click the checkbox to its right, scroll up the mouse wheel, and click the "Apply" button.

Click on the small triangle-shaped player button at the top of the scene again, and the cartoon boy will face us in the scene all the time and keep dancing the rumba.

What if we already have some generic animations designed for Unity Engine and want to reuse them on the cartoon boy?

Click the "Rig" tab in the "Inspector" window on the right, change the "Animation Type" to "Humanoid", click "Apply" button.

Delete the cartoon boy instance from the "Hierarchy" window and drag the cartoon boy icon to the "Hierarchy" window to create a new instance. In the "Inspector" window on the right, change the value of the "Y" channel of the "Rotation" from 0 to 180, so that the cartoon boy faces us.

Find any item in the generic animation resources designed for Unity Engine, such as the modern dance animation, click on the small triangle-shaped player like icon to the right of the icon, drag the animation represented by the cyan triangle icon onto the newly created instance, click on the small triangle-shaped player button above the scene, and the cartoon boy will dance the modern dance in the scene.

## Hands-on Tutorial on How to Import Rigify Character into Unreal Engine

Start "Unreal Editor", create a new directory in Unreal Explorer and rename it to "Rigify".

Drag and drop the exported "rigify-unreal.fbx" into this directory to bring up the "FBX Import Options" window, make sure "Skeleton" is "None", the checkbox next to "Import Morph Targets" is selected, and the checkbox next to "Import Animations" is selected, click the "Import" button, wait a moment, and the textures, models, skeletons and animations will be imported into this directory.

Double click on the "rigify-unreal_Anim" icon, it will automatically open the "Animation Editor", the cartoon boy is dancing rumba, and the colors show, everything is normal. Click the "Close" button on the "Animation Editor" to close it.

## Hands-on Tutorial on How to Retarget Animation to Rigify Character in Unreal Engine

If you drag the "rigify-unreal_Anim" icon to the front of the camera in the scene window to create an instance, click on the big triangular player button at the top of the scene and the cartoon boy will dance the rumba in the scene.

But the cartoon boy is facing us sideways, we need to change the value of the "Z" channel of the "Transform" column from 0 degrees to 90 degrees in the "Details" window on the right side. Click again on the large triangle-shaped player button at the top of the scene, and the cartoon boy will face us in the scene all the time and keep dancing rumba.

What if we already have some generic animations designed for Unreal Engine and want to reuse them on the cartoon boy?

Double-click the "rigify-unreal_Skeleton" icon to automatically open the "Skeleton Editor". Click the "Apply" button next to "Preview Mesh" under the "Animation" tab on the right. Click on the menu of "Window -> Retarget Manager" to display the "Retarget Manager" tab, click on the "Select Rig" drop-down box, select "Select Humanoid Rig", then click the "AutoMap" button for automatic bones mapping, most of the bones are mapped to the correct bones, but a small number of bones are mapped to the wrong bones and need to be corrected manually.

I have stored the mapping preset file of Rigify rig to Unreal rig on my website (https://www.mesh-online.net/BoneMapping.uasset), you can download it and copy it manually to the "Content/Rigify" directory of the Unreal Engine project. Go back to the "Skeleton Editor" and click the "Clear" button to completely clear the mapping you just generated automatically. Then click the "Load" button and select "BoneMapping", you can see that the bone mapping is correct now.

After fixing the bones mapping, click on the "Skeleton Tree" tab, right click on the root bone, select "Recursively Set Translation Retargeting Skeleton" in the popup menu, all the bones are set to "Skeleton" type, then set the "root" bone to "Animation" type, set the "DEF-spine" bone to "Animation Scaled" type.

When doing animation retargeting in Unreal Engine, we also need to adjust the initial pose of the skeleton to be similar to the initial pose of the source rig, for example, if the initial pose of the source rig is "A" and the initial pose of the cartoon boy's skeleton is "T", we need to rotate the two upper arms of the cartoon boy so that its initial pose is also "A".

In the "Skeleton Tree" tab, click the "DEF-upper_arm_L" bone, drag the rotation controller handle in the middle "3D View", and rotate the left arm so that the left arm points downward; click the "DEF-upper_arm_R" bone, drag the rotation controller handle in the middle "3D View", and rotate the right arm so that the right arm is pointing downward. Switch to the "Retarget Manager" tab, click the "Modify Pose" button below, and in the pop-up window, click "Use CurrentPose".

Click the "Save" button in the upper left corner to save the settings, and click the "Close" button on the "Skeleton Editor" to close the "Skeleton Editor".

In Unreal Engine's "Resource Management" window, find any item in the generic animation resources designed for Unreal Engine, such as modern dance animation, right click on it, select "Retarget Anim Assets -> Duplicate Anim Assets and Retarget" from the popup menu.", the animation retargeting interface will appear, select the "rigify-unreal_Skeleton" rig you want to retarget, click the "Retarget" button, and a new retargeted animation will be automatically generated for the rig.

If you drag the retargeted animation icon you just generated to the front of the camera in the scene window to create an instance, and click the large triangular-shaped player button at the top of the scene, the cartoon boy will dance a modern dance in the scene.

If you find that the animation looks wrong because the initial pose you just set is not suitable and you need to go back to fine-tune the initial pose, you can double-click the "rigify-unreal_Skeleton" icon again to automatically open the "Skeleton Editor" and switch to the "Retarget Manager" tab, click the "View Pose" button below and the last saved pose will be restored and you can continue to fine-tune the pose. Repeatedly test until the animation is perfect.

# Download 3D Character for Tutorial from the Mixamo Website

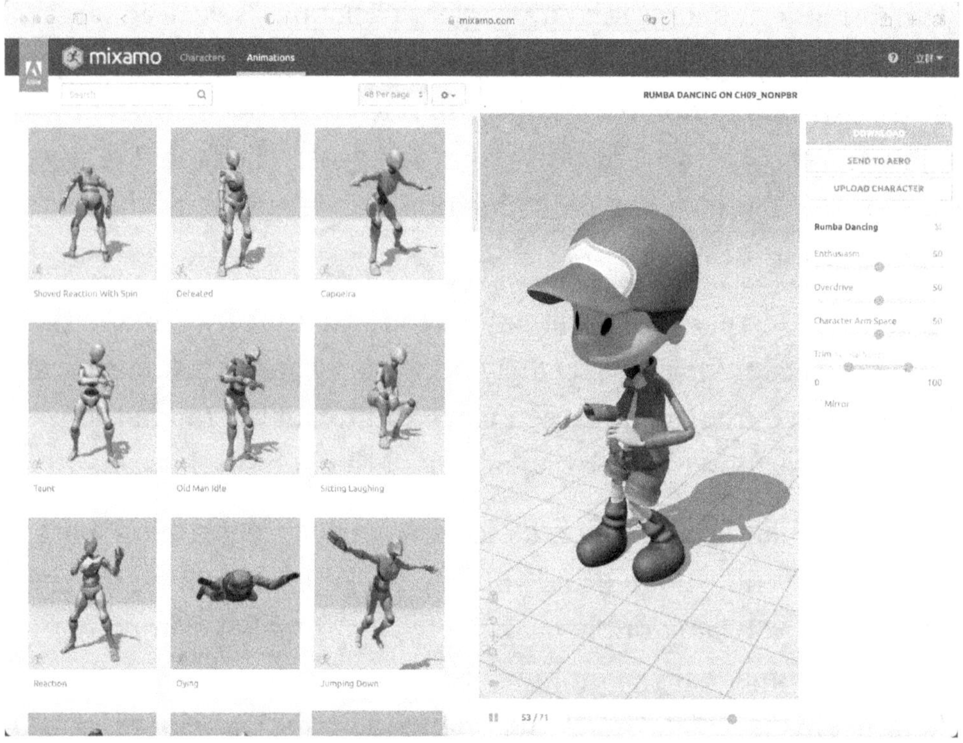

First, we go to the Mixamo website (https://www.mixamo.com/) to download a 3D character for tutorial purpose.

You need an Adobe account, if you don't have yet, you need to register one, after logging into your account, click on the "Characters" tab, find and click on the "Timmy" character; click on the "Animations" tab, find and click on the "Rumba Dancing" animation. Wait a moment, in the right 3D view, the cartoon boy Timmy will keep dancing rumba in a loop.

Click the "Download" button in the upper right corner of the page to bring up the "Download Settings" interface. The default setting is to download the 3D character in FBX format with animation, which is exactly what we need. Click on the "Download" button at the bottom right corner of the "Download Settings" interface. It will prompt you to wait a few moments and the download will begin shortly. Once downloaded locally, the filename will be "Rumba Dancing.fbx".

## Hands-on Tutorial on How to Bind Character with Auto-Rig Pro

We'll start our Auto-Rig Pro tutorial with the cartoon character we just downloaded, assuming you already have the "Auto-Rig Pro" add-on installed in Blender, because the "Auto-Rig Pro" add-on comes with the FBX exporting feature, so you don't need to install the "Better FBX Importer & Exporter" add-on.

First start Blender, press the "A" key in the "3D View" to select all objects in the scene, then press the "X" key, a small window will pop up next to the mouse to confirm the deletion, click "Delete", all objects in the scene will be deleted immediately.

Click the menu "File -> Import -> FBX", in the pop-up add-on parameter setting interface, expand the 'Armature' item, check the 'Automatic Bone Orientation' option, click the "Import FBX" button to import the character model.

Blender just started does not display textures by default, only the colors of the materials, so the 3D character's whole body is displayed as white, we need to switch to texture mode, click the down arrow icon to the right of several spherical icons in the upper right corner of the "3D View", it will show the current mode settings, click the "Texture" item under the "Color" section, you will find that the cartoon boy appears color on his body.

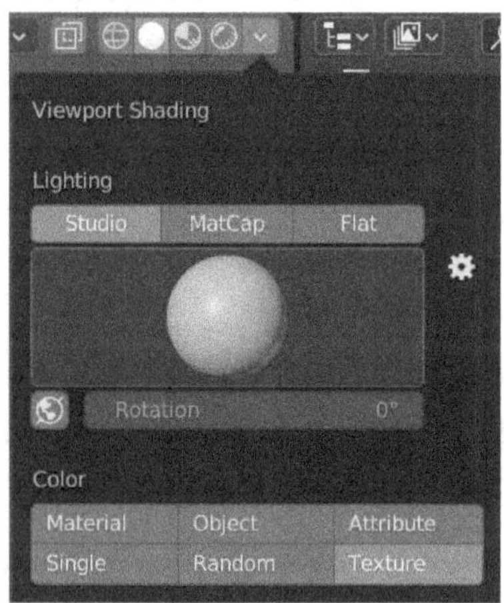

Click the "Skeleton" icon on the right side of the "Properties" window, expand the "Viewport Display" section, check the checkbox in front of "In Front", the armature will not be obscured by the body, always displayed in front.

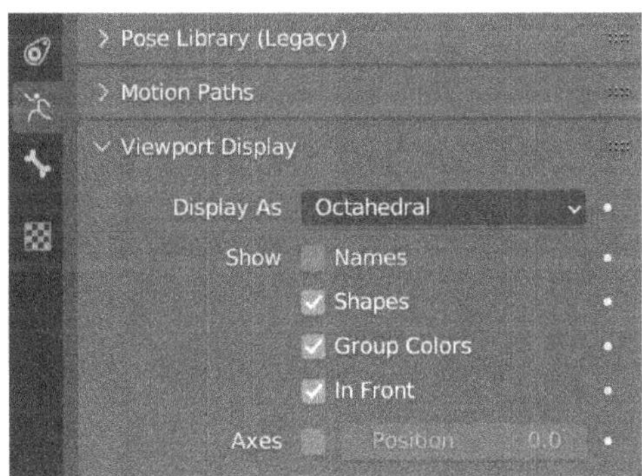

Drag the "Rotate", "Zoom" and "Pan" view controller on the right side of the "3D View" with the mouse to make the cartoon boy face the screen at the right size. Press the "Spacebar" key in the "3D View" and the cartoon boy starts animating. Since the cartoon boy's animation is only 72 frames long, and Blender starts with a default animation frame range of frame 1 to frame 250, frames 73 to 250 are stationary. Click on "End" in the "Timeline" window below, type 72 and press enter, the animation will loop between frame 1 and frame 72. Press the "ESC" key in the "3D View" to end the animation.

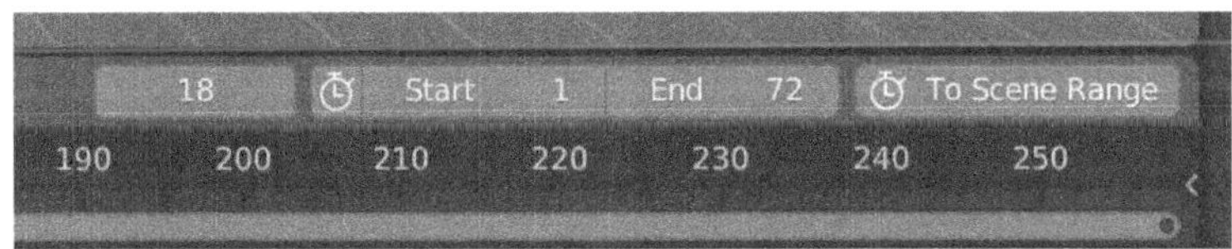

Here's what we're going to do, separate the cartoon boy from the armature as we bind it to the brand new Auto-Rig Pro rig.

The units in FBX are centimeters (cm), while the units in Blender are meters (m), a difference of 100 times. When importing the FBX file, the armature is virtually shrunk by a factor of 100, while the actual skeleton size and the actual model size are still 100 times the Blender default units.

We can do this by clicking on the character model, pressing the "Alt + P" key in the "3D View", and selecting "Clear and Keep Transformation" in the pop-up menu. But the pose remains the same as in the animation.

We then click the wrench-shaped icon in the "Properties" window on the right, switch to the "Modifier" window and find that the pose is retained because the "Armature" modifier has not been removed, click the "X" button to the right of the "Armature" modifier, you will find that the character becomes a "T" pose.

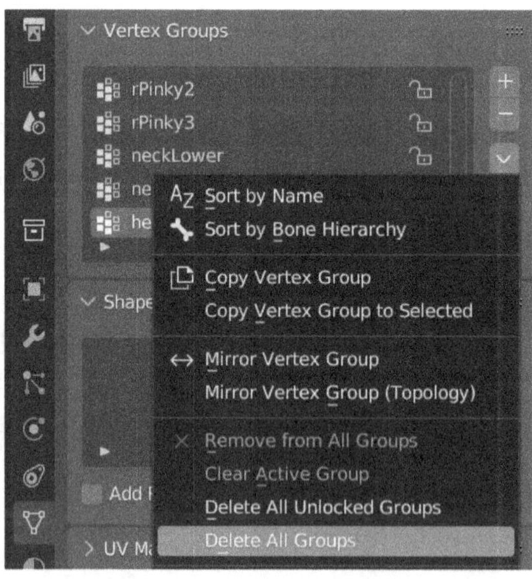

We click the green inverted triangle icon in the "Properties" window on the right, we will find that in the "Vertex Groups", there is still residual skinning information, click the down arrow on the right and select "Delete All Groups". and the remaining skinning information is deleted.

Finally, press the "Ctrl + A" key in the "3D View" and select "All Transforms", which will "apply" the translation, rotation and scaling. You can think of the "Apply" operation as writing the translation, rotation and scaling of the model as the vertex position inside the model, so that from the outside of the model, the model is at the origin, rotated to 0 and scaled to 1. The "Apply" operation is very important before doing binding and making animation in Blender.

After separating the character, the old armature is not really useful anymore, but instead of rushing to delete it, we hide it first, because it will still be useful when we do the animation retargeting in the next section, where we will retarget the animation to the brand new Auto-Rig Pro rig.

To hide the armature, you can click the small icon shaped like an eye on the armature item in the upper right corner of the outline view, or you can click the armature in the "3D View" and press the "H" key, both methods work.

After hiding the armature, only the cartoon boy is left in the scene. Let's start adding an "Auto-Rig Pro" rig.

Press the "N" key in the "3D View", the right sidebar will be shown, click the "ARP" tab, which is the "Auto-Rig Pro" interface.

Our workflow will use the semi-automatic alignment of the rig, so you need to expand the "Auto-Rig Pro: Smart" section, click the "Get Selected Objects" button, in the pop-up menu, the default is "Full Body", which is to generate the rig for the whole body, click the "OK" button, and the "Marker Point Interactive Placement" interface appears.

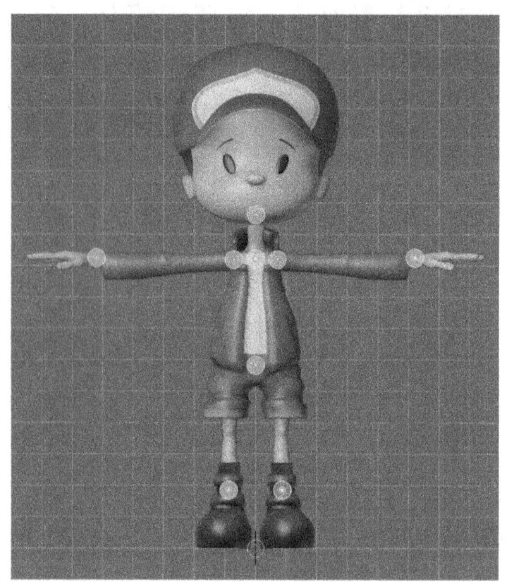

Click the "Add Neck" button, a circular marker will appear in the "3D View", move the mouse, the circular marker will move up and down, move it to the bottom of the neck, click the left mouse button to end the placement.

After the neck marker is placed, the button becomes "Add Chin" and place the marker point at the bottom of the chin in the same way.

Next are the shoulders, wrists, spine base, and the ankles, placing them on the corresponding parts of the cartoon boy.

Because this tutorial model is a cartoon style character with simple features, not even a mouth, there is no need to set facial marker points. If you need to set facial markers for a realistic character model in the future, you can click the "Facial Setup" button and the "3D View" will show a close-up of the face with markers for eyebrows, eyes, nose, cheeks, ears and chin already placed on it, and you need to move them to the right positions.

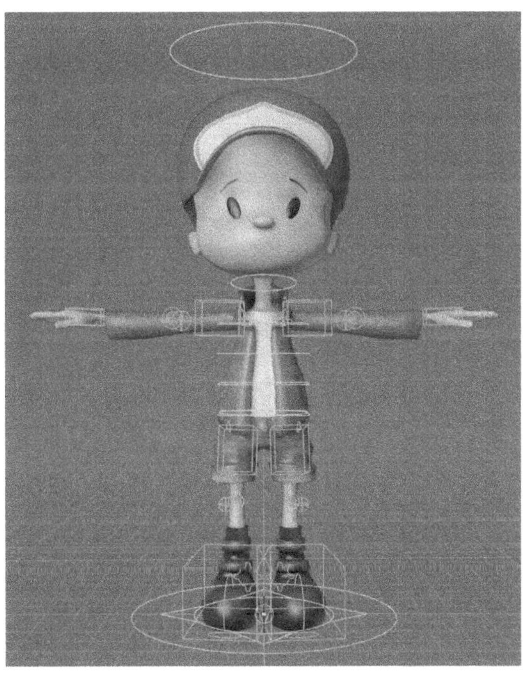

Uncheck the 'Fingers' option, click the "Go!" button, the mouse changes to the waiting state, wait a moment, the mouse changes to the normal state, and the "Match to Rig" button appears. Click on the "Match to Rig" button and something magical happens, the "Auto-Rig Pro" add-on automatically generates a new rig with controllers.

The newly generated rig with controllers is in "POSE" mode by default, press the "Ctrl + Tab" key to back to "OBJECT" mode. Select the newly generated rig with controllers, click the "Skeleton" icon in the "Properties" window on the right, expand "Viewport Display", click the checkbox in front of "In Front", so that the rig with controllers is always displayed at the top.

The last step is to bind the cartoon boy to the rig with controllers. Click in the "3D View" to select the character model, then hold down the "Shift" key and click to select the rig with controllers, the order in which you click is important.

Click on the "Skin" tab at the top of the "Auto-Rig Pro" interface to switch to the skinning window. The default skinning engine is "Heap Maps", which invokes Blender's built-in surface heat diffuse skinning algorithm.

There are more than one skinning engines, in addition to Blender's built-in skinning algorithm, there are also "Voxelized" and "Voxel Heat Diffuse Skinning (addon)".

The second algorithm simulates the heat diffuse process in space by generating a large number of point clouds inside the model, which runs very slowly and yields results close to those of voxel skinning.

The name of the third algorithm looks familiar, right? It looks like we've seen it before, it's actually the name of the voxel skinning add-on developed by myself. This feature was developed by the author of "Auto-Rig Pro" in cooperation with me. If you already have the "Voxel Heat Diffuse Skinning" add-on installed in Blender, you can set the skinning engine to the "Voxel Heat Diffuse Skinning (addon)" and the "Voxel Heat Diffuse Skinning" add-on will be called automatically when skinning.

Set the 'Engine' to 'Voxelized', click the "Bind" button, wait a few seconds and the skinning is done.

Here we test the skinning results, in the "3D View", click on the rig with controllers, press the "Ctrl + Tab" key to enter "POSE" mode, try to move the red-colored IK controller, the body will move with the controller and do the corresponding movement, the skinning result is good. After testing, press the "Ctrl + Tab" key again to exit "POSE" mode.

If you also have the "Voxel Heat Diffuse Skinning" add-on installed, you can also separately try the "Voxel Heat Diffuse Skinning" add-on from outside of Auto-Rig Pro again.

Click on the character model in the "3D View", then click on the rig with controllers. The voxel skinning add-on does not require the order of selection, either one can be chosen first.

Press the "N" key in the "3D View", the hidden right sidebar will be shown, click the "Mesh Online" tab, click the "Voxel Heat Diffuse Skinning" button, the add-on will report the progress in light blue text, wait a moment and the skinning will be finished.

Going into "POSE" mode again to test the skinning results, for this cartoon boy model, both skinning methods yield good results. But for more complex models, such as character models with many accessories of clothes and equipment, the two-stage skinning method of the voxel skinning add-on generates better skinning results.

## Hands-on Tutorial on How to Retarget Animation to Auto-Rig Pro Character

Auto-Rig Pro provides an "Animation Retargeting" module. Let's try to do animation retargeting with this built-in module and see how it works.

Expand the "Auto-Rig Pro: Remap" section, click on the "Source Armature" drop-down box and select the "Armature" rig, click "Target Armature" drop-down box, select the "rig" rig.

By clicking the "Auto Scale" button, the size of the two rigs becomes similar. When the animation is retargeted between rigs of similar size, the animation looks more natural, otherwise the movement may be too large or too small.

Click on the "Build Bones List" button to automatically generate the skeleton mapping. Because the "Mixamo" rig is a "famous" rig, Auto-Rig Pro does a good job of adapting it so that all bones are mapped correctly and do not need to be adjusted manually.

Scroll the mouse wheel and find the item "Target Bone" named "c_root_master.x" in the bone mapping list, click to select this item, then click the checkbox in front of "Set as Root" under the bone mapping list to mark it as the root bone.

Finally, click the "Re-Target" button on top of the bone mapping list, click the "OK" button in the pop-up menu, wait for a moment, and the animation retargeting is finished.

Press the "Spacebar" key to play the animation, the animation is exactly correct.

To prevent future problems when using ready-made add-ons to do animation retargeting, we then use a purely manual re-do of the animation retargeting, a method that can handle any complex rigs.

Recall from Chapter 4 that the secret to purely manually animation retargeting is to add a child bone to the source bone that has the exact same initial orientation as the target bone, and then constrain the target bone to the corresponding child bone. Because of the large number of bones, creating child bones with the exact same initial orientation as all the target bones is cumbersome. If we can make a copy of all the target bones, merge them into the source rig, and make them child bones of the corresponding source bones by adjusting the parent-child relationship of the bones, we can speed up this process.

Click on the rig with controllers, press the "Shift + D" key in the "3D View" and press the "Enter" key, this will duplicate an identical rig out.

To make it easier to see and manipulate the rig when merging it, we need to hide the controllers of the rig we just duplicated, and only

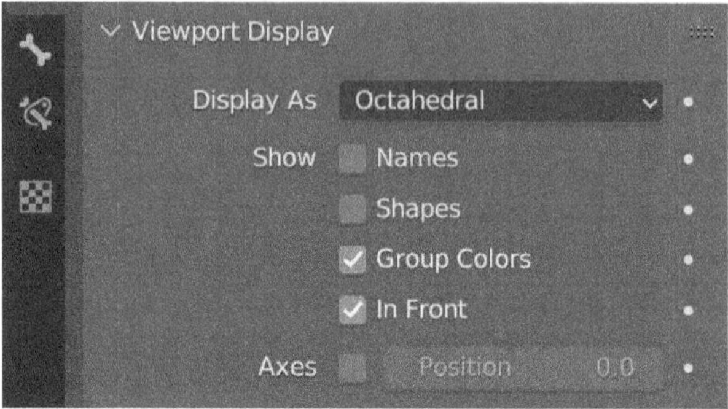


show the original shapes of the bones. Click the rig you just duplicated, click the "Skeleton" tab in the "Properties" window on the right, find the "Viewport Display" section, click the small triangle next to it to expand it, you can see that the "Shapes" item is enabled by default, which means that if the bone has a controller, only the controller of the bone will be displayed, hiding the original shape of the bone. Click the checkbox in front of "Shapes" to disable it, so that the bone does not show the controller, but only the original bone shape.

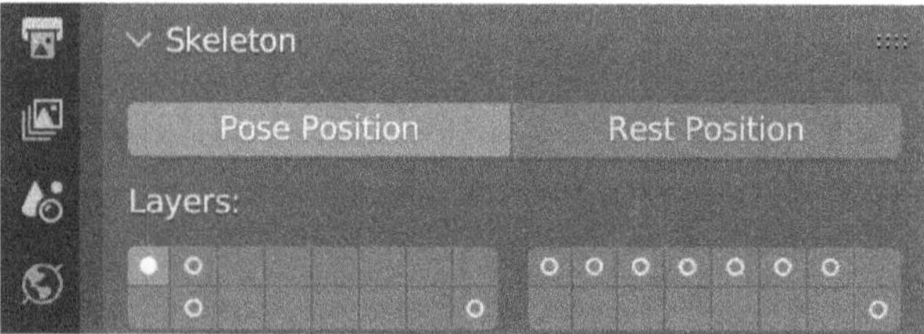


In the next step we delete all the other bones except the control bones. Click on the skeleton you just duplicated, click on the "Skeleton" tab in the "Properties" window on the right, and find the "Skeleton" section. Auto-Rig Pro's control bones are in the first layer, so we click on the first layer. In the "3D View", press the "Tab" key to enter "EDIT" mode, press the "A" key to select all the control bones, press the "H" key to hide all the control bones, press the "Tab" key again to exit "EDIT" mode. Hold "Shift" key and click to select all layers in "Pose Position" layer, press the "Tab" key to enter "EDIT"

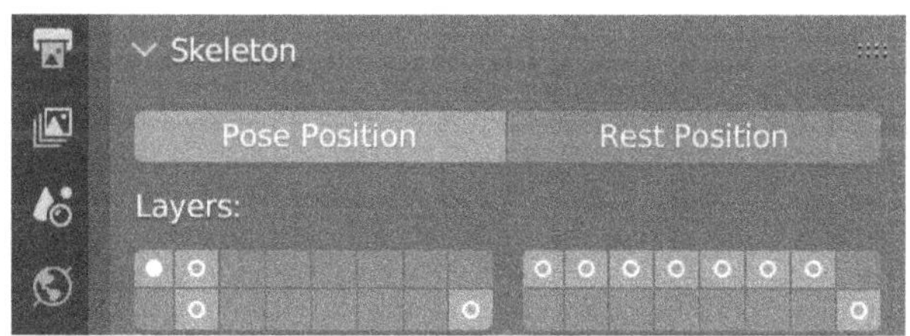

mode in the "3D View", press the "A" key to select all the unhidden bones, press the "X" key and click "Delete" in the pop-up window, then all the unhidden bones will be deleted. Press the "Alt + H" key to re-display all the control bones. In Auto-Rig Pro, the control bones include FK control bones, IK control bones, and Pole bones which control IK polar direction. Since we only need FK control bones, we can remove all other types of bones that we don't need, after deleting, press the "Tab" key again to exit "EDIT" mode.

Before merging the skeletons, there is one more problem to solve, we need to clean up the residual constraint information on the control bones, otherwise, it will cause unpredictable interference to the animation retargeting. In the "3D View", press the "Ctrl + Tab" key to enter "POSE" mode, press the "A" key to select all the control bones, select menu "Pose -> Constraints -> Clear Pose Constraints", all the constraints on the control bones will be cleared. Press the "Ctrl + Tab" key again to exit "POSE" mode.

When merging armatures in Blender, the two armatures must have the same rotation, otherwise, it will bring issue. Since the rotation of the original armature is 90 degrees, while the rotation of the new rig is zero, we need to rotate the original armature to zero, then rotate the new rig to match the pose of the original armature and apply rotation, so the rotations of the two rigs are both zero. Now we can merge the two rigs into one rig. Click in the "3D View" to select the rig you just duplicated, then hold down the "Shift" key and click to select the source rig, the order of clicking is very important, then press the "Ctrl + J" key, the duplicated rig will be merged into the source rig. After merging the two rigs, rotate the original armature to the former pose.

We find that the newly merged FK control bones have disappeared, this is because the source rig only shows the first layer by default, while the merged FK control bones are in the other layers, we need to show all layers. Click on the source rig, click on the "Skeleton" tab in the "Properties" window on the right, find the "Skeleton" section, hold down the "Shift" key and click on all the layers in the "Pose Position" layer, and all the bones in all the layers will be displayed.

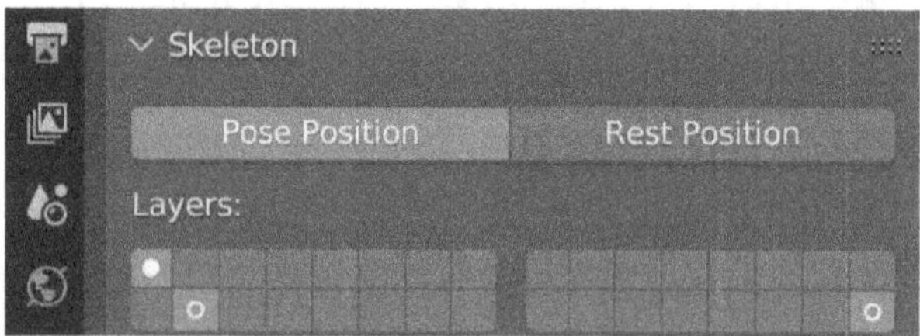

The next task is to adjust the parent-child relationship of the bones, so that the merged control bones becomes the children of the corresponding source bones. In the "3D View", press the "Tab" key to enter "EDIT" mode, click to select a new merged bone, then hold down the "Shift" key and click to select the corresponding source bone, press the "Ctrl + P "key, select "Keep Offset" in the pop-up menu, and the new merged bone will become a child bone of the selected source bone. Repeat the above steps until all the new bones become children bones of the corresponding source bones, and press the "Tab" key again to exit "EDIT" mode.

If you press the "Spacebar" key to play the animation, you will see that all the merged control bones follow the source bones. If you find that some bones are not following, it means that it was forgotten and you need to go back and re-add it as a child bone of the corresponding source bone.

The next task is to add constraints to the bones so that the target bone exactly copies the motion of the source bone. We first add a "Copy Rotation" constraint to every FK control bone to achieve an exact copy of the rotation motion. Click on the rig with controllers in the "3D View", press the "Ctrl + Tab" key to switch to "POSE" mode, click on the "Constraints" tab in the "Properties" window on the right, and add a "Copy Rotation" constraint to every FK control bone. "Target" is set to the source rig, and "Bone" is set to a child bone with the same name on the source rig. Press the "Ctrl + Tab" key to exit "POSE" mode.

Bones with only the "Copy Rotation" constraint can only be animated in place, like the torso pinned to a wall, and cannot move up and down, so we also need to add a "Copy Location" constraint for the root bone, so that the whole rig can follow the up and down motion of the root bone. Click on the rig with controllers in the "3D View", press the "Ctrl + Tab" key to switch to "POSE" mode, click on the "Constraints" tab in the "Properties" window on the right, and add a "Copy Location" constraint to the "c_root_master_x" bone, "Target" is set to the source rig, and "Bone" is set to a child bone with the same name on the source rig. Press the "Ctrl + Tab" key to exit "POSE" mode.

Press the "Spacebar" key to play the animation and you will find that the cartoon boy's limbs look like they are held in place by ropes, only his torso is twisting, what is going on? This is because Auto-Rig Pro is working in IK mode by default, we need to switch to FK mode. Click on the rig with controllers, press the "Ctrl + Tab" key in the "3D View" to enter "POSE" mode, click to select any bone on a limb, such as the left forearm bone, in the "Tool" tab of the right sidebar, find the "Rig Main Properties" section, drag the mouse to the right side of the "IK-FK Switch" item to make the value 1.0, or click on the "IK-FK Switch" item and directly enter "1" and press the "Enter" key. Repeat the above steps to switch all four limbs from IK mode to FK mode.

Press the "Spacebar" key to play the animation, the animation is perfect.

## Hands-on Tutorial on How to Export Auto-Rig Pro Character

If you export the animation of a retargeted animation implemented by constraint directly, you will find that there is no animation data. Why is this? The reason is that there must be an "Action" in Blender's "Animation Manager" for the FBX add-on to think there is animation data to export. So we need to create an "Action" first.

Click the "Skeleton" tab in the "Properties" window on the right, find the "Skeleton" section, and hold down the "Shift" key to click to select the first and the second layers in the "Pose Position" layer.

Click on the rig with controllers, press the "Ctrl + Tab" key in the "3D View" to enter "POSE" mode, press the "A" key to select all the control bones. Pull the timeline slider to frame 1, press the "I" key in the "3D View", and select "Location, Rotation & Scale" in the pop-up menu; pull the timeline slider to frame 72, press the "I" key, select

"Location, Rotation & Scale" in the pop-up menu, press the "Ctrl + Tab" key again to exit "POSE"mode.

The above operation will generate an "Action" in the "Animation Manager" with a start frame of 1 and an end frame of 72.

If you export an animation generated by Auto-Rig Pro's built-in "Animation Retargeting" module, you can skip the above step because it has already automatically baked an "Action" of 1 to 72 frames.

Next, we use Auto-Rig Pro's built-in FBX export module to export FBX files.

In the "3D View", click and select the cartoon boy, then hold down the "Shift" key and click to select the rig with controllers, expand the "Auto-Rig Pro: Export" section to bring up the exporter settings window, where you can select "Unity" for the game engine and "Universal" for the skeleton, click the checkbox in front of "Selected Objects Only", switch to the "Misc" tab, click the checkbox in front of "Embed Textures", select a directory where you want to store the exported FBX files, enter the filename "arp-unity.fbx", click the "Auto-Rig Pro FBX Exp..." button, and you will export a file with the name "arp-unity.fbx" that is suitable for Unity Engine.

Click again in the "3D View" to select the cartoon boy, then hold down the "Shift" key and click to select the rig with controllers, expand the "Auto-Rig Pro: Export" section to bring up the exporter settings window, where you can choose "Unreal Engine" for the game engine and "Universal" for the skeleton, and click the checkbox in front of "Selected Objects Only", switch to the "Misc" tab, click the checkbox in front of "Embed Textures", select a directory where you want to store the exported FBX files, enter filename "arp-unreal.fbx", click the "Auto-Rig Pro FBX Exp..." button, and it will export a file with the name "arp-unreal.fbx", which is suitable for Unreal Engine.

## Hands-on Tutorial on How to Import Auto-Rig Pro Character into Unity Engine

Start the "Unity Editor", create a new directory in "Unity Explorer" and rename it to "ARP".

Drag the exported "arp-unity.fbx" into this directory and wait a moment for an icon to appear with a colorless cartoon boy image on top and a small triangle-shaped player like icon on the right, indicating that it contains animations.

Click on this icon, click on the "Materials" tab in the "Inspector" window on the right, click on the "Extract Textures..." button, a pop-up window will appear asking for the directory to release the textures, the default is the current directory, click "Choose", wait a moment, the textures will be released to the current directory, the cartoon boy in the icon shows the color.

We will also find another popup window in "Unity Editor" titled "NormalMap settings", indicating that a material is being used as a normal map and that the texture must be marked as a normal map in the import settings. Click the below "Fix now" button to let "Unity Editor" fix it automatically.

## Hands-on Tutorial on How to Retarget Animation to Auto-Rig Pro Character in Unity Engine

If you click on the "Rig" tab in the "Inspector" window on the right, you will see that the "Animation Type" is "Generic", which means that the animation type contained in the FBX file is a user-defined "normal" format, which can only be used for the corresponding skeleton in FBX.

If you drag the icon to the "Hierarchy" window to create an instance, then click on the small triangle-shaped player like icon to the right of the icon, drag the "root|rigAction" animation of the cyan triangle icon to the instance you just created, and click on the small triangle-shaped player button at the top of the scene, the cartoon boy will dance the rumba in the scene.

But the cartoon boy has his back to us, and the rumba stops after one dance. We need to change the value of the "Y" channel of "Rotation" from 0 to 180 in the "Inspector" window on the right, and then click on the icon of the cartoon boy in "Unity Explorer", click on the "Animation" tab in the "Inspector" window on the right, find the "Loop Time" item, click the checkbox to its right, scroll up the mouse wheel, and click the "Apply" button.

Click on the small triangle-shaped player button at the top of the scene again, and the cartoon boy will face us in the scene all the time and keep dancing the rumba.

What if we already have some generic animations designed for Unity Engine and want to reuse them on the cartoon boy?

Click the "Rig" tab in the "Inspector" window on the right, change the "Animation Type" to "Humanoid", click "Apply" button.

Delete the cartoon boy instance from the "Hierarchy" window and drag the cartoon boy icon to the "Hierarchy" window to create a new instance. In the "Inspector" window on the right, change the value of the "Y" channel of the "Rotation" from 0 to 180, so that the cartoon boy faces us.

Find any item in the generic animation resources designed for Unity Engine, such as the modern dance animation, click on the small triangle-shaped player like icon to the right of the icon, drag the animation represented by the cyan triangle icon onto the newly created instance, click on the small triangle-shaped player button above the scene, and the cartoon boy will dance the modern dance in the scene.

## Hands-on Tutorial on How to Import Auto-Rig Pro Character into Unreal Engine

Start "Unreal Editor", create a new directory in Unreal Explorer and rename it to "ARP".

Drag and drop the exported "arp-unreal.fbx" into this directory to bring up the "FBX Import Options" window, make sure "Skeleton" is "None", the checkbox next to "Import Morph Targets" is selected, and the checkbox next to "Import Animations" is selected, click the "Import" button, wait a moment, and the textures, models, skeletons and animations will be imported into this directory.

When the import is complete, a "Message Log" window pops up, displaying a warning message.

"Please make sure to enable the 'Export Smoothing Groups' option in the FBX Even for tools that don't support smoothing groups, the FBX Exporter will generate appropriate smoothing Even for tools that don't support smoothing groups, the FBX Exporter will generate appropriate smoothing data at export-time so that correct vertex normals can be inferred while importing."

This English paragraph means that the FBX file is missing smoothing group information. Let's ignore this warning message for now, because Unreal Engine will automatically generate smoothing groups from normals when importing FBX files, so it won't cause display errors.

Click the "Close" icon on the "Message Log" window to close it.

Double click the "arp-unreal_Anim" icon, it will automatically open the "Animation Editor", the cartoon boy is dancing rumba, but the color display seems not normal, the whole body is made of metal. Click the "Close" button on the "Animation Editor" to close it.

Double click on the material sphere, it will automatically open the "Material Editor" and we find that the "Metallic" channel and "Roughness" channel are wrong, which is caused by the difference between Blender's material system and Unreal Engine's material system. After manually fixing the two channels, click the "Save" button in the upper left corner to close the "Material Editor".

Double-click the "arp-unreal_Anim" icon again and the "Animation Editor" will open automatically, with the cartoon boy dancing the rumba and the colors showing normally. Click the "Close" button on the "Animation Editor" to close it.

## Hands-on Tutorial on How to Retarget Animation to Auto-Rig Pro Character in Unreal Engine

If you drag the "arp-unreal_Anim" icon to the front of the camera in the scene window to create an instance, click on the big triangular player button at the top of the scene and the cartoon boy will dance the rumba in the scene.

But the cartoon boy is facing us sideways, we need to change the value of the "Z" channel of the "Transform" column from 0 degrees to 90 degrees in the "Details" window on the right side. Click again on the large triangle-shaped player button at the top of the scene, and the cartoon boy will face us in the scene all the time and keep dancing rumba.

What if we already have some generic animations designed for Unreal Engine and want to reuse them on the cartoon boy?

Double-click the "arp-unreal_Skeleton" icon to automatically open the "Skeleton Editor". Click the "Apply" button next to "Preview Mesh" under the "Animation" tab on the right. Click on the menu of "Window -> Retarget Manager" to display the "Retarget Manager" tab, click on the "Select Rig" drop-down box, select "Select Humanoid Rig", then click the "AutoMap" button for automatic bones mapping, most of the bones are mapped to the correct bones, but a small number of bones are mapped to the wrong bones and need to be corrected manually.

I have stored the mapping preset file of Auto-Rig Pro rig to Unreal rig on my website (https://www.mesh-online.net/ BoneMapping2.uasset), you can download it and copy it manually to the "Content/ARP" directory of the Unreal Engine project. Go back to the "Skeleton Editor" and click the "Clear" button to completely clear the mapping you just generated automatically. Then click the "Load" button and select "BoneMapping", you can see that the bone mapping is correct now.

After fixing the bones mapping, click on the "Skeleton Tree" tab, right click on the root bone, select "Recursively Set Translation Retargeting Skeleton" in the popup menu, all the bones are set to "Skeleton" type, then set the "root" bone to "Animation" type, set the "root_x" bone to "Animation Scaled" type.

When doing animation retargeting in Unreal Engine, we also need to adjust the initial pose of the skeleton to be similar to the initial pose of the source rig, for example, if the initial pose of the source rig is "A" and the initial pose of the cartoon boy's skeleton is "T", we need to rotate the two upper arms of the cartoon boy so that its initial pose is also "A".

In the "Skeleton Tree" tab, click the "arm_stretch_l" bone, drag the rotation controller handle in the middle "3D View", and rotate the left arm so that the left arm points downward; click the "arm_stretch_r" bone, drag the rotation controller handle in the middle "3D View", and rotate the right arm so that the right arm is pointing downward. Switch to the "Retarget Manager" tab, click the "Modify Pose" button below, and in the pop-up window, click "Use CurrentPose".

Click the "Save" button in the upper left corner to save the settings, and click the "Close" button on the "Skeleton Editor" to close the "Skeleton Editor".

In Unreal Engine's "Resource Management" window, find any item in the generic animation resources designed for Unreal Engine, such as modern dance animation, right click on it, select "Retarget Anim Assets -> Duplicate Anim Assets and Retarget" from the popup menu.", the animation retargeting interface will appear, select the "arp-unreal_Skeleton" rig you want to retarget, click the "Retarget" button, and a new retargeted animation will be automatically generated for the rig.

If you drag the retargeted animation icon you just generated to the front of the camera in the scene window to create an instance, and click the large triangular-shaped player button at the top of the scene, the cartoon boy will dance a modern dance in the scene.

If you find that the animation looks wrong because the initial pose you just set is not suitable and you need to go back to fine-tune the initial pose, you can double-click the "arp-unreal_Skeleton" icon again to automatically open the "Skeleton Editor" and switch to the "Retarget Manager" tab, click the "View Pose" button below and the last saved pose will be restored and you can continue to fine-tune the pose. Repeatedly test until the animation is perfect.

# About the Author

He graduated from the Department of Electronic Engineering of University of Electronic Science and Technology of China in 1991, majoring in telemetry and remote control, but found that his main interest was in the field of software development and showed a high talent, so he took the path of independent developer without any hesitation.

He had independently developed a 3D game engine and used his own 3D game engine to develop and publish the casual game "3D Safari Park" for iPad in Apple App Store.

He had developed an editor extension plugin "Mantis LOD Editor" for Unity Engine to simplify 3D models, which is very popular among users.

He had developed the heavyweight "Voxel Heat Diffuse Skinning" add-on and the very best-selling "Better FBX Importer & Exporter" add-on for Blender, helping Blender to get out of the island of game development by himself.

In this book, the author describes in detail how to use Blender instead of 3ds Max and Maya for the game development workflow, and learners can focus on one area of the workflow according to their interests.

Each chapter ends with a series of entrepreneurship classroom topics, where the author relates the experiences and lessons learned in his twenty years of independent development, pointing out the pitfalls that independent developers and small teams tend to encounter, and giving straightforward solutions.

By studying this book, you will find that financial freedom is not unattainable for independent developers if you do well enough.

Whether you are a graduating college student, an independent developer just starting out, or a small team with little money, you can learn from this book and help your business succeed.